RAIL CENTRES:
DERBY

RAIL CENTRES:
DERBY

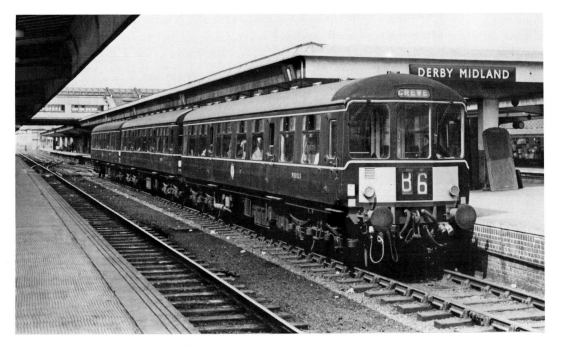

BRIAN RADFORD

Nottingham

Booklaw Publications

Contents

Previous page, opposite:
**Derby Midland station in 1891 before the
alterations which added the new booking halls
and the two-storey office block in front of the
original Thompson buildings.**
MR Official, Author's Collection

and
**Three car diesel multiple-unit at platform 2 at
Derby Midland waiting to depart to Crewe with
a stopping train on 8 June 1962.** *P. J. Lynch*

First published 1986 by Ian Allan Ltd

This edition published 2007 by Booklaw Publications
382, Carlton Hill, Nottingham NG4 1JA

ISBN 1-901945-17-0

Printed by
The Amadeus Press, Cleckheaton, West Yorkshire

Front cover, top:
**Gresley Class D3 4-4-0 No 4302 stands at the west
end of Derby Friargate station with a train from
Nottingham on 27 June 1933.** *H. C. Casserley*

Rear cover, top:
**LMS Fowler Class 4F 0-6-0 No 44042 with an
empty stock train rounds the curve from
Chaddesden past Derby Junction signalbox to
pass over the Five Arches bridge and into Derby
station on 24 May 1959.** *R. C. Riley*

Rear cover, bottom:
**Class 31 diesel-electric locomotive No 31152
accelerates past the rear of Derby Midland
station with an empty steel train on 10 April
1974.** *Barry J. Nicolle*

Front endpaper:
**'Jubilee' class 4-6-0 No 45626 *Seychelles* moves
empty stock from platform No 6 at Derby
Midland on 31 August 1963 on a Works Open Day
as evidenced by the crowd of spotters on the
Hulland Street entrance bridge which gave
access to both No 4 shed and the machine and
paint shops.** *T. Boustead*

Rear endpaper:
**A BR/Sulzer 1Co-Co1 No D39 entering Derby
Midland station past Derby Station North
signalbox with a train from Leeds on 10 March
1963.** *P. H. Wells*

Acknowledgements and abbreviations

Acknowledgements

My thanks to G. A. Yeomans for allowing me to quote freely from his two privately published monographs on the Great Northern lines in Derbyshire and the Derby to Melbourne and Ashby lines, and to the following for providing information: Denis Peacock, Ken Palmer, John Palmer, Peter Bilson, Peter Rowbotham, Lawrence Knighton, Maurice Gregory, Peter Taylor, Leslie Askin, Vic Forster, and to the staff of the local History Section of Derbyshire County Libraries at Derby and the staff of the Technical Library at the Railway Technical Centre, Derby.

Vic Forster and Lawrence Knighton also read the manuscript and made many helpful suggestions.

For assistance with photographic material my thanks go to the Ian Allan Library, Brian Waters keeper of Derby's Industrial Museum, the National Railway Museum, Ron Buckley, Glyn Waite, Vic Forster, Roger Carpenter, Dick Riley, Nelson Twells, David Tee, the Public Relations & Publicity Officer, BREL and the British Railways Board.

My special thanks to Cynthia Radford who quickly rendered my handwritten manuscript into a readable typescript — no mean feat!

J. B. Radford

Dedication
This book is dedicated to my son Stephen.

Abbreviations

APT	Advanced Passenger Train
B&DJR	Birmingham & Derby Junction Railway
FO	Fridays only
FSX	Fridays and Saturdays excepted
FX	Fridays excepted
GNR	Great Northern Railway
G&SWR	Glasgow & South Western Railway
GWR	Great Western Railway
HST	High Speed Train
LD&ECR	Lancashire, Derbyshire & East Coast Railway
LMR	London Midland Region
LMSR	London, Midland & Scottish Railway
L&BR	London & Birmingham Railway
L&NWR	London & North Western Railway
LNER	London & North Eastern Railway
L&SWR	London & South Western Railway
MBM&MJR	Manchester, Buxton, Matlock & Midlands Junction Railway
M&GNR	Midland & Great Northern Joint Railway
MCR	Midland Counties Railway
MGR	Merry-go-round
MMR	Melbourne Military Railway
MR	Midland Railway
MX	Monday excepted
N&DJR	Newcastle & Darlington Junction Railway
NMR	North Midland Railway
NSR	North Staffordshire Railway
S&DJR	Somerset & Dorset Joint Railway
SR	Southern Railway
SO	Saturdays only
SX	Saturdays excepted
WCML	West Coast main line
Y&NMR	York & North Midland Railway

Conversion Tables

Old pence	New pence
1	½
2	1
3	
4	1½
5	2
6	2½
7	3
8	3½
9	4
10	
11	4½
12	5

Shillings	Pence
1	5
2	10
3	15
4	20
5	25
6	30
7	35
8	40
9	45
10	50

Early railway development (1778-1849)

Derby became a city as late as 1977 when Her Majesty, Queen Elizabeth II, conferred that status upon it by Letters Patent in her Jubilee year, but it has a history going back to before Roman times as a settlement on the banks of the River Derwent. The Romans set up a garrison at Little Chester which they called 'Derventio'. It became a Royal Borough at the time of Edward the Confessor and its population rose from a thousand in AD1000 to some 11,000 by 1800 and by the beginning of the 20th century had some 115,000 inhabitants of whom no fewer than 10,000 worked for the Midland Railway Co.

When Daniel Defoe visited the town he styled it 'one of gentry rather than of trade' but within a century all that was to change with the coming of the railways. In the wake of the railway came firms such as Rolls-Royce, Aiton & Co Ltd, International Combustion Ltd, Qualcast Ltd and Fletcher & Stewart whilst firms such as William Bemrose, printers, and Joseph Mason, paint manufacturers were able to expand considerably as Derby grew to be an important railway centre.

The first 'railways' in the Derby area were simple tramways with a line of rails made of wooden frames such as that laid in 1778 between Shipley Colliery and the nearby canal. The first use in England of flanged iron rails laid above ground was at Wingerworth, some distance north of Derby, where Joseph Butler laid rails to carry coke and iron-ore to his furnaces in 1788. Nearer Derby the Little Eaton gangroad opened in May 1795 to carry coal, stone and pottery from Smithy Houses, Denby, to a spur of the Derby Canal at Little Eaton. Teams of horses were used to haul wagons

Left:
Part of the Little Eaton gangroad at Denby Colliery seen here after closure on 29 September 1908. *MR Official, Author's Collection*

Below:
The yearly 'right of way' journey being undertaken along the Ticknall tramway on 23 May 1911. *MR Official, Author's Collection*

with loaded containers which were then lifted bodily off by crane into canal barges: this line remained open until July 1908. The three-armed Derby Canal referred to above was completed in 1795 to link with the Trent & Mersey Canal at Swarkestone and the Erewash Canal at Sandiacre, after which navigation up the Derwent as far as Derby ceased.

Nearer to Derby on the south side a tramway, built in 1811-12, linked alabaster quarries at Aston-on-Trent with the Trent & Mersey Canal between Aston Lock and Shardlow. It went out of use before World War 1.

The nearest tramway to Derby was that built to link the Kilburn Colliery Co's Stanley Colliery with a coal distribution depot in Chaddesden some 3½ miles away. Loaded wagons ran down from the pit by gravity but a winding house in Chaddesden hauled the empty wagons back to the summit. Many children (and others!) have hitched a lift on this tramway, saving themselves the ½d fare from Derby to West Hallam by the Great Northern line, although the state of their clothes sometimes resulted in eventual retribution!

Main line railways in the Derby area post-dated the Stockton & Darlington, Liverpool & Manchester and the Canterbury & Whitstable lines, for it was not until after the Leicester & Swannington line had opened in the summer of 1832 and cheaper coals at 10s per ton began arriving in Leicester, that the Nottinghamshire and Derbyshire coal-masters realised that they must consider a similar scheme to link their pits with that city of lose some of their markets.

Accordingly the weekly meeting of the Erewash coal-masters held at the Sun Inn, Eastwood, on 16 August 1832 resulted in a scheme to lay a railway from their collieries to Leicester. By November 1834 the scheme had been detailed in a much developed form as a set of lines to link Nottingham and Derby with Leicester and thence to join the L&BR line at Rugby.

Derby was to be a terminus with a proposed station in Derwent Street on the site of what was then Darby's Yard, with a bridge constructed to carry the line over the Derwent near the site of the present Exeter Bridge.

However, this original scheme was to be much modified by proposals put forward by an entirely separate group of railway promoters who, in October 1835, proposed the construction of a line of railway from Derby to Birmingham with a link with the L&BR at Hampton-in-Arden by means of the Stonebridge branch from Whitacre Junction. This branch was deleted from the Birmingham and Derby scheme in return for the deletion of the MCR proposed extension from Pinxton to connect with the NMR's proposed line at Clay Cross. However, the Birmingham & Derby solicitors surreptitiously put through their Stonebridge branch proposals under a separate Act on the same day and once passed, the two companies were then united to form the Birmingham & Derby Junction Railway by Act of Incorporation dated 19 May 1836.

The B&DJR intended to connect 'end-on' with a third railway, the NMR, a line 72 miles long connecting Leeds and the manufacturing centres and mineral wealth of the areas along its route with Derby and thus the Midlands; a terminus for which was to be provided near to the Nottingham Road on the edge of Derby town centre. It was to be a line which the *Derby Mercury* newspaper observed would 'make Derby a centre of communication and must, we imagine, increase the trade and importance of the town', as indeed it eventually did.

The direct connection between the NMR and B&DJR lines was given approval at a public meeting held in Derby Town Hall in December 1835 with the Mayor, Richard Wright Haden Esq, presiding, but the full Town Council had other ideas, remembering the MCR proposal of a separate terminus on a different site, and in February 1836 suggested that a joint station for all three companies should be built on The Holmes, an area of low-lying pastureland to the south of the town and skirted by the River Derwent. A deputation was sent to meet the chairmen of the two

Below:
Early plan of Derby Works and the station in relation to land to be acquired, dated 1839.
Author's Collection

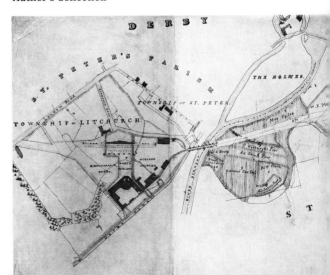

principal companies together with George Stephenson, who was involved in both railways, and others, but because of the susceptibility of the site to flooding the Council's proposals were dismissed and an alternative site much nearer to the town centre on Castle Fields was suggested by the railway deputation.

First evidence of the combined tripartite station scheme which was eventually adopted appears in a letter sent by John Fox Bell, secretary to the MCR to Henry Patterson, a director of the North Midland. Dated 13 November 1835 it reads as follows:

'I am directed by our Board to send you, according to your request, the inclosed tracing of our proposed terminations at Derby. Which will be adopted is not yet decided.
I remain Sir,
Yours faithfully,
J. F. Bell, Secretary'

The plan enclosed showed the two alternative

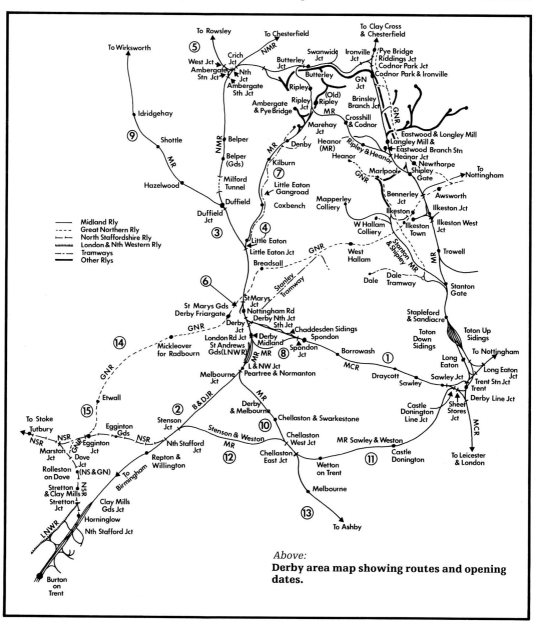

Above:
Derby area map showing routes and opening dates.

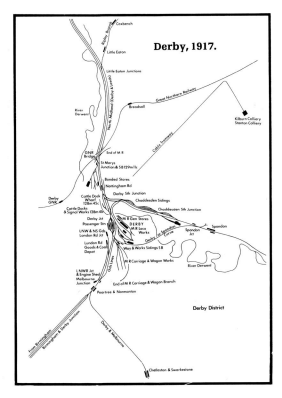

Derby, 1917.

Derby area map showing routes and opening dates. 1. MCR Derby to Nottingham opened 30 May 1839; **2.** B&DJR Derby to Hampton Junction opened 5 August 1839; **3.** NMR Derby to Masboro' opened 11 May 1840; **4.** Little Eaton Branch opened 1848; **5.** MBM&MJR Ambergate to Rowsley opened 4 June 1849; **6.** St Mary's Branch opened September 1855; **7.** Ripley Branch opened 1 September 1856; **8.** Spondon Curve opened 27 June 1867; **9.** Wirksworth Branch opened 1 October 1867; **10.** Derby and Melbourne Branch opened 1 September 1868; **11.** Sawley and Weston plus the section to Chellaston East Junction opened 6 December 1869; **12.** Chellaston West Junction to Stenson Junction opened 3 November 1873; **13.** Melbourne to Worthington opened 1 October 1869 and Worthington to Ashby opened 1 January 1874; **14.** GNR Nottingham London Road to Etwall opened for goods 28 January 1878; **15.** GNR Nottingham London Road to Tutbury opened for passengers 1 April 1878.

sites then under consideration for the station at Derby, ie: the one near the town centre and the other in The Holmes. The major disadvantages of the town centre site was its limited size and the fact that by its location, it could not offer through communication and would have to be a terminus only.

After the Derby Council agreed to make a better roadway to The Holmes site, agreement

was reached in June 1838 that this plan should be adopted.

In February 1839 Francis Thompson of Derby was appointed by the NMR to 'prepare plans for the stations and in executing the works at a salary of £400pa during the period his services are required'. He was not only to be responsible for Derby station but also for the other splendid stations along the line to Leeds.

Plots of land were purchased in the adjacent Castle Fields for railway purposes and by March 1839 plans had been published showing the station building which was to serve all three companies, and the polygonal engine shed of the NMR. These were soon followed by comprehensive plans of the workshops and sheds of all three companies.

On 9 April 1839 the NMR Committee agreed that tenders be invited by 21 May for the Derby station contract and five were received. Thomas Jackson of Pimlico, London, was awarded the job at a price of £39,986 of which the B&DJR and the MCR companies agreed to contribute £4,796 and £4,923, respectively and agreed to pay rent at 6% per annum on the proportion of the costs for their accommodation.

Seventeen drawings were involved of which four were for the NMR polygonal engine house and the two workshops which flanked it as oblique wings.

The main station building, with a facade 1,050ft long, was dominated by a bold projecting central block with a Venetian window above the entrance. The main two-storied office block was 14 windows wide, those on the ground floor being semi-circular headed and those on the first floor square

Below:
Print of an old lithograph of the tri-junct station at Derby as it originally appeared when completed in 1840. *BR, LMR, Author's Collection*

Above:
Lithograph of the interior of Derby station about 1840. The three bay train shed can be clearly seen with the inset MCR platform face on the right. The locomotive workshops of the NMR are on the left and the engine shed of the MCR on the extreme left. Notice the railway policemen or 'bobby' hand signalling the locomotive shunting operation. *BR, LMR, Author's Collection*

Below:
The oldest known photograph of Derby station taken about 1860, with the Locomotive and Carriage & Wagon Works in the foreground. *Midland Railway Official, Author's Collection*

headed with corbelled sills. The elevation tailed off symmetrically each side in an arcaded screen wall, punctuated by subsidiary entrances for goods vehicles, cattle, etc.

The three bay glazed train shed was 34ft high at the apexes and the roof was supported on 60 graceful reeded and bonded hollow cast-iron columns which also acted as rain-water pipes. A single platform ran the entire length of the facade with a 31ft wide projecting central face to serve NMR trains and inset faces, 15ft 6in wide, at south (west) and north ends to serve the B&DJR and MCR trains respectively, each company thereby being unhindered by any other. These tracks were punctuated at intervals by small hand-operated turntables large enough for one four-wheeled carriage to be turned and transferred to other locations by means of lines set at intervals and running across the main through lines, the remainder of the train shed at that time being used both for storing carriages and for dealing with goods and other traffic. Lighting was provided by means of no less than 216 gas lamps, two on each of the 60 roof support columns and the remainder on 40 stone lamp columns set along the platform at intervals.

Construction of the three lines proceeded contemporaneously, work on the B&DJR commencing in August 1837 on the NMR in February 1837 and on the MCR in May 1837. The bridges over the Derby Canal and the River Derwent, later known as the Five Arches, had been commenced and by mid-summer 1838 all the necessary land had been acquired.

The NMR route, which largely took the line of the valleys and had a maximum gradient of 1 in 330 (except for a short distance south of Clay Cross tunnel) cost in all around £3 million involved 28 contracts, had some 200 bridges, seven tunnels and 26 stations, and took three years to complete. The first section from Masborough to Derby opened on 11 May 1840 when the first NMR train starting from Masborough was joined there by the through carriages of the Sheffield & Rotherham Co's 5.30am service from its Wicker station to Derby. The train was 65min late at Chesterfield, where George Stephenson and George Hudson climbed aboard, and eventually reached Derby at 9.30am, 1hr 45min late.

Right:
Artist's impression of Milford Tunnel, just beyond Duffied, soon after completion for the NMR. Note the 'bobby' signalling a train through on its way to Derby. *BR, LMR, Author's Collection*

Below:
North Midland Railway timetable for January 1841.

North Midland Railway.

TIME TABLE FOR PASSENGER TRAINS.----JANUARY 1st, 1841.

Stations.	No.	1	2	3	4	5	6	7	Sundays.				
DOWN TRAINS.		1st & 2nd Class.	1st, 2d & 3rd Class.	1st, 2d & 3rd Class.	1st & 2nd Class.	1st & 2nd Class.	1st, 2d & 3rd Class.	1st, 2d & 3rd Class.	1st & 2nd Class.	1st, 2d & 3rd Class.	1st, 2d & 3rd Class.	1st, 2d & 3rd Class.	1st, 2d & 3rd Class.
Departure from	Miles.	Mail. P. M.	Mail. A. M.	A. M.	A. M.	A. M.	A. M.	A. M.	Mail. P. M.	Mail. A. M.	A. M	A. M.	P. M.
LONDON	...	8.30	...	...	6. 0	9.30	...	11. 0	8.30	...	...	8. 0	...
Birmingham	...	...	3.15	6.45	10.30	1. 0	...	...	...	3.15	...	...	...
		A.M.	A. M.	A. M.	P. M.	P. M.	P. M.	P. M.	A. M.	A. M.	A. M.	P. M.	P. M.
DERBY	0	3.39	6. 0	9.30	1. 0	3.45	4. 0	6. 0	3.39	6. 0	8. 0	3. 0	6. 0
Arrival at BELPER	7¼	...	6.21	9.51	1.21	...	4.21	6.21	...	6.21	8.21	3.21	6.21
AMBER GATE (For Matlock, &c.)	10½	...	...	10. 3	1.33	...	4.33	6.33	...	...	8.33	3.33	6.33
WINGFIELD (For Alfreton & Mansfield.)	14	...	6.38	10.15	1.45	...	4.45	6.45	...	6.38	8.45	3.45	6.45
Chesterfield	24	4.47	7. 2	10.43	2.13	4.42	5.13	7.13	4.47	7. 2	9.13	4.13	7.13
ECKINGTON	30¼	...	7.17	10.58	2.28	...	5.28	7.28	...	7.17	9.28	4.28	7.28
BEIGHTON	34	...	7.27	11.11	2.41	...	5.41	7.41	...	7.27	9.41	4.41	7.41
MASBRO' and Rotherham	40	5.34	7.42	11.24	2.54	5.13	5.54	7.54	5.34	7.42	9.54	4.54	7.54
SHEFFIELD	45	5.47	8. 0	11.45	3.15	5.30	6.15	8.15	5.47	8. 0	10.15	5.15	8.15
Ditto Departure,	45	5.15	7.30	11. 0	2.30	5. 0	5.30	7.30	5.15	7.30	9.30	4.30	7.30
SWINTON (For Doncaster.)	45	...	8. 1	11.45	3.15	...	6.15	8.15	...	8. 1	10.15	5.15	8.15
DARFIELD	49¼	...	8.13	11.58	3.28	...	6.28	8.28	...	8.13	10.28	5.28	8.28
BARNSLEY	53	6.12	8.24	12.11	3.41	5.50	6.41	8.41	6.12	8.24	10.41	5.41	8.41
WAKEFIELD	60	6.34	8.39	12.32	4. 2	6. 9	7. 2	9. 2	6.34	8.39	11. 2	6. 2	9. 2
NORMANTON (Manchester & York Junction.)	63	...	8.47	12.40	4.10	...	...	...	...	...	...	...	...
WOODLESFORD	68	...	9. 3	1. 0	4.30	...	7.30	9.30	...	9. 3	11.30	6.30	9.30
Arrival at LEEDS	72¾	7. 8	9.30	1.30	5. 0	7. 0	8. 0	10. 0	7. 8	9.30	12. 0	7. 0	10. 0
		A.M.	A. M.	P. M.	P. M.	P. M.	P. M.	P. M.	A. M.	A. M.	A. M.	P. M.	P. M.
Hebden-Bridge	90	...	...	2.50	...	...	...	...	...	...	...	...	...
YORK	87	7.42	10.15	2.15	5.45	7.45	...	...	7.42	10.15	...	7.45	...
HULL	111	9.30	...	...	...	...	...	...	9.30	...	...	...	...

Stations.	No.	1	2	3	4	5	6	7	Sundays.				
UP TRAINS.		1st, 2d & 3rd Class.	1st, 2d & 3rd Class.	1st & 2nd Class.	1st & 2nd Class.	1st, 2d & 3rd Class.	1st, 2d & 3rd Class.	1st & 2nd Class.	1st, 2d & 3rd Class.	1st, 2d & 3rd Class.	1st, 2d & 3rd Class.	1st, 2d & 3rd Class.	1st & 2nd Class.
Departure from	Miles.	A. M.	A. M.	A. M.	A. M.	P. M.	P. M.	Mail. P. M.	A. M.	P. M.	P. M.	P. M.	Mail. P. M.
HULL	...	...	...	6.45	9.30	...	2. 0	4.45	...	...	...	...	4.45
YORK	...	...	6.30	8.45	11. 0	...	4. 0	6. 0	7. 0	...	4. 0	...	6. 0
Hebden-Bridge	...	...	...	7.45	...	1. 0	3.15 MAIL.	...	...	...	... MAIL.	...	...
		A. M.	A. M.	A. M.	A. M.	P. M.	P. M.	P. M.	A. M.	P. M.	P. M.	P. M.	P. M.
LEEDS	0	6.15	7.15	9.30	11.45	2.30	4.45	6.40	7.45	1. 0	4.45	5. 0	6.40
Arrival at WOODLESFORD	4¾	6.30	7.30	...	12. 0	2.45	...	...	8. 0	1.15	...	5.15	...
NORMANTON (Manchester & York Junction)	9¾	...	...	9.54	...	3. 2	5. 9	...	...	...	...	...	...
WAKEFIELD	12¾	7. 2	8. 2	10.11	12.32	3.17	5.26	7.17	8.32	1.47	5.26	5.47	7·17
BARNSLEY	19¾	7.23	8.23	10.28	12.53	3.38	5.43	7.36	8.53	2. 8	5.43	6. 8	7.36
DARFIELD	23½	7.34	8.34	...	1. 4	3.49	...	...	9. 4	2.19	...	6.19	...
SWINTON (For Doncaster.)	27¾	7.47	8.47	...	1.17	4. 2	5.55	...	9.17	2.32	5.55	6.32	...
MASBRO' and Rotherham	32¾	8. 2	9. 2	10.57	1.32	4.17	6.12	8.19	9.32	2.47	6.12	6.47	8.19
SHEFFIELD	37¾	8.30	9.30	11.15	2. 0	4.45	6.30	8.40	10. 0	3.15	6.30	7.15	8.40
Ditto Departure	37¾	7.45	8.45	10.45	1.15	4. 0	6. 0	8. 0	9.15	2.30	6. 0	6.30	8. 0
BEIGHTON	38¾	8·21	9.21	...	1.51	4.36	...	...	9.51	3. 6	...	7. 6	...
ECKINGTON	42½	8.37	9.37	...	2. 7	4.52	...	...	10. 7	3.22	...	7.22	...
Chesterfield	48¾	8.58	9.58	11.42	2.28	5.13	6.57	9. 4	10.28	3.43	6.57	7.43	9. 4
WINGFIELD (For Alfreton & Mansfield.)	58¾	9.26	10.26	...	2.56	5.41	...	...	10.56	4.11	...	8.11	...
AMBER GATE (For Matlock, &c.)	62¼	9.35	10.35	...	3. 5	5.50	...	...	11. 5	4.20	...	8.20	...
BELPER	65½	9.43	10.43	...	3.11	5.58	...	...	11.13	4.28	...	8.28	...
Arrival at DERBY	72¾	10.15	11.15	12.45	3.45	6.30	8. 0	10. 9	11.45	5. 0	8. 0	9. 0	10. 9
		P. M.	P. M.	P. M.	P. M.	P. M.	P. M.	A. M.	P. M.	P. M.	P. M.	P. M.	A. M.
Birmingham	120	...	2. 0	4.30	6.15	...	10.45	...	...	7.45	10.45	...	...
LONDON	204	5.45	6.45	8. 0	11.15	...	...	5.30	7.15	...	...	...	5.30

FARES FOR PASSENGERS, HORSES, CARRIAGES, &c.

DERBY TO	Passengers. 1st. Class.		2d. Class.		3rd Class.		Carriages		Horses. One.		Two.		Three.	
	s.	d.	s.	d.	s.	d.	s.	d.	s.	d.	s.	d.	s.	d.
SHEFFIELD	11	0	7	0	3	6	30	0	20	0	35	0	45	0
LEEDS	18	0	12	0	6	0	45	0	30	0	50	0	65	0
YORK	21	0	14	6	...	...	65	0	45	0	75	0	95	0
HULL	24	0	16	6	...	...	85	0	60	0	95	0	125	0

☞ Persons riding in their own Carriages are charged Second Class Fares.

Trains leave **Leeds for Manchester** Dewsbury, Huddersfield, Halifax, Todmorden, Rochdale, &c. at 7.45 a.m., 10.0 a.m., 1.0 p.m., and 3.0 p.m.

For **York and Hull** at (7.0 a.m. Mail Train for Hull only) 8.0 a.m., 10.45 a.m., 3.15 p.m., and 5.45 p.m.

All the Trains, (excepting No. 2,) are in communication at **Derby** with Trains to **Nottingham and Leicester.**

Passengers by the No. 2 Train may proceed from Leeds to London in the third Class Carriages, arriving in London at 7.0 p.m., and leaves London for Leeds at 7.0 a.m. (Sundays excepted) Fare 20s. 6d. each.

Coaches in direct connection with Nos. 1, 2, and 5 Down Trains to Newcastle and Edinburgh, *via* Harrogate, Ripon, and Durham.

Passengers are particularly requested to notice the *Number of the Carriage* on which their Luggage is placed.

Parcels &c., are conveyed by all the Trains, and are received at all the principal Coach-offices in the Kingdom.—Charges for Parcels under 14 lbs. Weight from London to Leeds, York, and Hull, 2s. 6d. each, including delivery.

Carriage Trucks and Horse Boxes are kept at all the principal Stations; but to prevent disappointment, it is recommended that Notice be given the day previous to their being required.

Post Horses are always in readiness at the **Derby and Leeds** Stations on the arrival of the various Trains.

TIME IS ALLOWED AT DERBY FOR REFRESHMENT.

By Order, **H. Patteson, Secretary.**

[PRINTED BY WM. BEMROSE, DERBY.]

Above:
The NMR viaduct which crossed both the Derby Canal and the Nottingham Road on its way from Derby (to the left) to the north. It is seen here in this contemporary view drawn about 1842.
BR, LMR, Author's Collection

However, the first down train, comprising four 1st and two 2nd class coaches hauled by two locomotives and with Robert Stephenson on the footplate of the pilot engine, left Derby on time at 9.15am and reached Masborough to schedule.

Completion of the line to Leeds was delayed by a few weeks and it officially opened throughout on 30 June 1840. On this occasion bands played on the platforms at Cudworth, Chesterfield and Belper and upon arrival at Derby, guests tucked into a 'cold collation with wine' served on two enormous tables spread out along the platform which was tastefully decorated with evergreens. That same evening the NMR directors entertained their guests to dinner at the Music Hall in Albion Street, Derby, 'several hundred ladies' attending the event with George Carr Glyn, chairman of the company presiding.

After the official opening, public services began on the following day, Wednesday, 1 June 1840 with a service of six trains daily each way between Derby and Leeds. The 1st class fare from Derby to Leeds was 18s and the 2nd class fare 12s. Traffic became heavy almost immediately and on one particular day in July four NMR trains totalling 86 coaches in all, reached Euston station, London, during the busiest day of the week, the heaviest however being cleared in 10min.

The first 'Mail' train from London Euston to Sheffield ran through Derby on 16 June 1840 and the service was extended to York from 19 August, while the 'Midland TPO' service, initially between Rugby and Newcastle, followed in June 1845, changing to Tamworth-Derby in 1852 and then Bristol-Derby in 1855.

Construction of the MCR line, the Act for which received Royal Assent on 21 June 1836, involved four main contracts of which the sections from Derby to Long Eaton and Long Eaton to Leicester were let to William Mackenzie of Liverpool, formerly confidential assistant to Thomas Telford. Work was put in hand with equal enterprise and speed and by the spring of 1838 some 3,500 men and 328 horses were at work. Charles Vignoles, the engineer, had 14 miles of track laid on blocks of Derbyshire millstone grit each of 5cu ft, whilst the remainder was laid on larch sleepers 3ft 9in apart. 550,000cu yd of earthworks were necessary, the deepest cutting being 30ft and the highest embankment 20ft. Railway construction work at Spondon, near Derby, was to have involved suspending navigation on the Derby Canal at a cost of £2 per hour, but by a stroke of fate it had to be drained for repairs at a fortuitous moment and by concentrating all the labour force of two or three hundred men night and day, the local populace turning out in force to see the show, the railway works were completed before the canal could be re-opened, the contractor thus being saved the expense of paying for closure.

The line duly became the first of the three to open and on Thursday, 30 May 1839 the first of four official trains left Nottingham at 12.30pm comprising four 1st class and two 2nd class coaches decorated with flags and hauled by Jones Turner & Evans 2-2-0 *Sunbeam* to cheers from the assembled multitudes and accompanied by the sound of 'God Save The Queen' played by the Regimental Band of the 5th Dragoon Guards. The second train, hauled by Butterley built 2-2-0 'Ariel', left 5min later and accomplished the run to Derby, a distance of 15½ miles in 45min, an average speed of 21mph, the return trip being even faster at an average speed of 30mph a sensation quite unknown to the local populace of that day!

The section of line to Loughborough and Leicester opened on 4 May 1840 and the first official trip along the section from Leicester to

Below:
The local press announcements of the opening of the NMR and MCR. *Author's Collection*

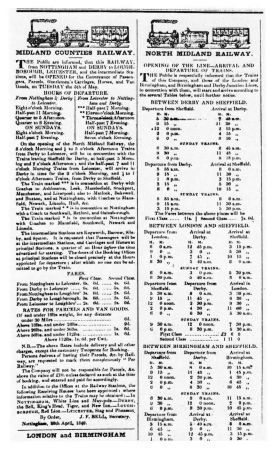

Rugby, where the line joined the L&BR, was made on 18 May 1840, public opening following on 30 June. Thus the Derby public had a through route to the capital and could arrive at the splendid Euston station, terminus of the L&BR.

The B&DJ line officially opened between Derby and Hampton Junction, a distance of 38½ miles, on Monday, 5 August 1839 without public ceremony. A party of directors boarded the nine-coach train at Birmingham's Curzon Street station and were hauled by the new Taylor 2-2-2 *Birmingham* along the L&B line as far as Hampton Junction where the train reversed for the run along the new line to Derby. Various stops were made to inspect stations and other locations and the train eventually entered the B&DJR platform at Derby station at 2pm where it was greeted with cheers from assembled spectators. A 'sumptuous cold collation' followed at the King's Head Hotel under the auspices of Mr Wallis, the proprietor.

Ordinary traffic on the line began a week later on Monday, 12 August 1839 with an initial weekday service of five trains each way to Birmingham and an extra one at Hampton only, whilst on Sundays there were but three. Services were revised when the direct line to Birmingham from Whitacre was opened in February 1842. Fares from Derby to Birmingham were 10s 1st class, 7s 2nd and 5s 3rd class, with a journey time by the best train of 2hr 15min.

Initial services on the MCR amounted to five trains on weekdays and two on Sundays, the fastest train between Derby and Nottingham taking a mere 25min to do the trip, non-stop. Fares were 3s 6d 1st class, 2s 2nd and 1s 3rd class. Third class passengers could, however, only book tickets at Derby or Nottingham.

On the NMR line from 1 January 1843 a service of five trains ran on weekdays in each direction between Derby and Leeds in a best time of 3hr and 20min and there were three trains on Sundays. In addition there was a mail train leaving Derby at 2.53am and arriving at Leeds at 5.53am with a return service leaving Leeds at 7.9pm and arriving at Derby at 10.18pm. There were also two goods trains to and from Leeds, one daily goods train each way to and from Manchester via Normanton, three coal trains from Clay Cross to Derby, returning empty and one coke train running between Masborough and Derby.

However, for all three railways now opened with lines radiating from Derby dividends were decidedly disappointing and in addition a ruinous competition had set in between the

Midland Counties Railway.

HOURS OF DEPARTURE.

AUGUST 1, 1842.

DOWN TRAINS

No. of Trains.	1	2	3	4	5	6	1 (Sun)	2 (Sun)	3 (Sun)	4 (Sun)
Class	1,2,3	1&2	1&2	1,2,3	1&2	1&2	1,2,3	1&2	1,2,3	1&2
DEPART FROM	a m	a m	a m	a m	a m	p m (Mail)	a m	a m	p m	p m (Mail)
London		6 0	9 15	11 0	5 0	9 0		8 0		9 0
Birmingham		8 30		1 15	6 0					
Coventry		9 12		2 4	6 45					
Rugby	6 45	9 45	12 50	2 50	8 40	12 20	7 30	12 15	6 0	12 20
Ullesthorpe	7 5	10 0	1 10	3 10	9 0	12 40	7 50	12 35	6 20	12 40
Broughton	7 15	10 8		3 18			8 0		6 30	
Wigston	7 25	10 20		3 30			8 12		6 42	
Leicester	7 45	10 40	1 45	3 50	9 30	1 10	8 30	1 10	7 0	1 10
Syston	7 58	10 50	2 0	4 5	9 40	1 25	8 45	1 25	7 15	1 25
Sileby	8 6	11 0		4 15			8 54		7 24	
Barrow	8 13	11 5		4 25			9 2		7 32	
Loughboro'	8 20	11 15	2 18	4 35	10 0	1 45	9 10	1 45	7 40	1 45
Kegworth	8 32	11 25	2 30	4 50	10 12		9 22	2 0	7 52	
ARRIVE AT										
Nottingham	9 15	12 10	3 15	5 30	10 50	4 10	10 0	2 30	8 30	4 10
Derby	9 0	12 10	3 15	5 30	10 50	2 49	10 0	2 30	8 30	2 49
Sheffield	11 45	2 45	5 30	8 15		5 0		5 30		5 0
Leeds	1 15	4 0	7 0	9 45		6 19		7 15		6 19
York	3 0	4 45	7 45			6 40		7 30		6 40
Darlington	5 15	7 0				9 25				9 20
Hull	3 45	6 45				8 30		8 50		8 36
Manchester	5 0	6 20	8 45			8 40		9 30		

UP TRAINS

No. of Trains.	1	2	3	4	5	6	1 (Sun)	2 (Sun)	3 (Sun)	4 (Sun)
Class	1,2,3	1&2	1,2,3	1&2	1,2,3	1&2	1,2,3	1&2	1,2,3	1&2
DEPART FROM	a m	a m	a m	p m	p m (Mail)	a m	a m	p m	p m (Mail)	
Manchester			7 0	10 0		4 45				
Hull			6 15	10 40		4 55			5 0	
Darlington			6 15	9 15		3 30			8 30	
York			8 45	12 0		6 19		6 45	6 19	
Leeds		6 0	9 30	1 0		7 0		7 30	7 0	
Sheffield		7 30	10 45	1 50		8 12		8 45	7 9	
Derby	8 15	10 30	1 15	4 40	7 30	10 40	6 45	12 15	7 0	10 40
Nottingham	8 15	10 30	1 15	4 40	7 30	9 0	6 45	12 15	7 0	9 0
Kegworth	8 50	11 0	1 48	5 13	8 5		7 25	12 45	7 35	
Loughboro'	9 2	11 10	2 0	5 25	8 17	11 26	7 39	1 0	7 47	11 20
Barrow	9 13				8 28		7 49		7 58	
Sileby	9 20	11 30			8 35		7 55		8 5	
Syston	9 30	11 30	2 20	5 45	8 45	11 45	8 1 20		7 55	11 45
Leicester	9 50	11 50	2 40	6 0	9 0	12 0	8 30	1 40	8 30	12 0
Wigston	10 0				9 10		8 40		8 40	
Broughton	10 15				9 25		8 58		8 55	
Ullesthorpe	10 36	12 15	3 15	6 30	9 40	12 30	9 10	2 10	9 10	12 30
ARRIVE AT										
Rugby	11 0	12 50	3 40	7 0	10 0	12 50	9 30	2 30	9 30	12 50
Coventry	12 35	1 34	6 26	9 2	12 27					
Birmingham	1 20	2 30	7 45	10 15	1 30					
London	3 15	6 0	7 45	11 15		5 0	1 30	7 30		5 0

NOTTINGHAM TO DERBY

DEPART FROM	1,2,3	1&2	1&2	1,2,3	1&2	1,2,3	1,2,3 (Sun)	1&2 (Sun)
	a m	a m	p m	p m	p m	a m	p m	p m
Nottingham	7 20	10 40	2 45	6 0	9 0	9 0	7 0	9 0
Beeston	7 29	10 49	2 54	6 9	9 9	9 9	7 9	9 9
Long-Eaton	7 38	10 58	3 3	6 18		9 18	7 18	9 9
Sawley	7 46	11 5	3 11	6 26	9 23	9 26	7 26	9 23
Borrowash	7 55	11 15	3 20	6 35		9 35	7 35	9 9
Spondon		11 20		6 40		9 40	7 40	
ARRIVE AT								
Derby	8 5	11 25	3 30	6 45	9 40	9 45	7 45	9 40

DERBY TO NOTTINGHAM

DEPART FROM	1&2	1,2,3	1&2	1,2,3	1,2,3	1&2 (Sun)	1,2,3 (Sun)
	a m	a m	p m	p m	p m	a m	p m
Derby	3 30	9 0	1 30	4 50	7 40	3 30	9 15	8 0
Spondon		9 5	1 35	4 55			9 20	8 5
Borrowash		9 11	1 41	5 3	7 53		9 26	8 11
Sawley		9 20	1 50	5 10	8 0		9 33	8 20
Long-Eaton		9 28	1 58	5 26	8 10		9 43	8 28
Beeston		9 37	2 7	5 28	8 18		9 52	8 37
ARRIVE AT								
Nottingham	4 10	9 45	2 15	5 35	8 25	4 10	10 0	8 45

. Third Class Carriages will be attached at Leicester to the Down Train No. 1, and detached at that place from the Down Train No. 2. Also, be detached at Leicester from the Up Train No. 1, excepting on Saturdays, when they will be attached at Leicester to the Up Train No. 4, calling at all the intermediate Stations except Wigston.

[J. BURTON, PRINTER, HAYMARKET, LEICESTER.]   BY ORDER, J. F. BELL, Secretary.

Above:
MCR timetable dated 1 August 1842.
MR Official, Author's Collection

MCR and B&DJR who were in direct competition for traffic between Derby and London, for at that time almost all of the traffic from north-eastern England passed along the NMR line on its way south.

The MCR line was shorter as a route to London, but the NMR tended to favour the smaller B&DJR company for George Stephenson had been closely involved in the promotion of both schemes. Also, since NMR men handled all the traffic arriving in Derby from the north, they could do a lot to influence its onward transmission southwards!

For three years intending travellers made merry as both the MCR and B&DJR companies cut fares stage by stage in an attempt to secure traffic for their particular line. The MCR protested in vain that the B&DJR had not declared themselves to be in competition, as required by Parliamentary Standing Orders, but had promoted the line merely as a link between east and west. At one stage the B&DJR were carrying passengers with through tickets between Derby and London for only 2s 1st class and 1s 6d 2nd class between Derby and Hampton Junction, a distance of 38 miles, whereas other passengers were forced to pay 8s and 6s respectively if they were not travelling on to London! The MCR took the B&DJR to court at the Queen's Bench and obtained a ruling that all passengers must be charged the same.

Eventually the controversy drew to a close, for the B&DJR announced that, with an earnest desire to develop resources and reduce the cost of working their line, they had approved a proposal by the NMR for the amalgamation of the three lines of railway which centre in Derby, as a measure that would be highly beneficial to them all. The whole subject was considered by the proprietors and terms agreed.

At a shareholders' meeting held in November 1842 an NMR Committee of Enquiry had recommended severe economies which included the sale of 'surplus' rolling stock and

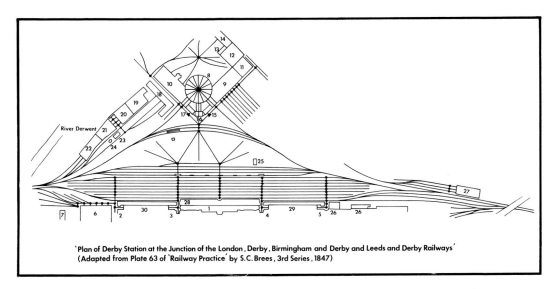

'Plan of Derby Station at the Junction of the London, Derby, Birmingham and Derby and Leeds and Derby Railways'
(Adapted from Plate 63 of 'Railway Practice' by S.C. Brees, 3rd Series, 1847)

other money-saving schemes, but Newton and fellow directors objected on the grounds that public safety would be affected. Newton and his colleagues then left the meeting and afterwards George Hudson was appointed a director of the NMR, and it was he who perceived that amalgamation was the key to salvation for the three companies.

Following the low of the period up to the summer of 1843, the London money market underwent important changes, railway shares again became buoyant and railway promotion a solution to investment. Thus in the improved financial climate the 'Great Midland Amalgamation Bill' received Royal Assent on 10 May 1844 and the Midland Railway Co was born. Hudson himself took the first general half-yearly meeting at Derby on 16 July of that year and a policy of urgent expansion and improvement was initiated all of which was, in one way or another, to affect Derby as a railway centre and increase its importance. Local expansion schemes included the building of part of the extension along the Erewash Valley between the old Long Eaton station and Codnor Park, this section being opened on 6 September 1847, soon followed by further sections to Pye Bridge, Pinxton and Mansfield (the latter embracing the 1819 Mansfield and Pinxton line), opened on 9 October 1849, the final link northwards to Clay Cross being opened for goods traffic in 1861 and for passenger traffic on 1 May 1862.

On the Erewash Valley line extensive sidings at Toton opened in 1855 and that curious interchange station, Trent, on 1 May 1862 whilst nearer to Derby itself a branch line opened from Little Eaton Junction reaching

Above:

Derby station diagram 1847.

1. Buildings for the ticket office and waiting rooms; **2.** Place for removing post-chaises or special carriages passing from Derby to Leeds; **3.** Place for forwarding post-chaises or special vehicles; **4.** Place for taking on post-chaises or special carriages going from Derby to London or Birmingham; **5.** Place for removing post-chaises or other special carriages passing from London or Birmingham; **6.** Building for the goods traffic; **7.** Goods office; **8.** Large rotunda for housing the engines. (Originally NMR, Author's note.); **9.** Workshop for repairing engines with two storeys. (Originally NMR, Author's note.); **10.** Workshop for repairing carriages. (Originally NMR, Author's note.); **11.** Forges. (Originally NMR, Author's note.); **12. and 13.** Forges and furnaces for re-heating the tyres of wheels. (Originally NMR, Author's note.); 14. Pay office. (Originally NMR, Author's note.); **15.** Offices. (Originally NMR, Author's note.); **16.** Entrance. (Engines also entered by the two other tracks). (Originally NMR, Author's note.); **17.** Depot. (Originally NMR, Author's note.); **18.** Sheds for carriages. (Originally MCR, Author's note.); **19.** Building of two storeys to house and paint the carriages. (Originally MCR, Author's note.); **20.** Workshops for building carriages. (Originally MCR, Author's note.); **21.** Shed for carriages. (Originally MCR, Author's note.); **22.** Shed for engines. (Originally MCR, Author's note.); **23.** Coke depot; **24.** Reservoir; **25.** Small office; **26.** Sheds; **27.** Shed. (For B&DJR locomotives, Author's note.); **28.** Departure platform for Leeds, London and Birmingham; **29.** Not in original key list but was originally the B&DJR platform. (Author.); **30.** Arrival platform for passengers from the south (London) or west (Birmingham). (This was originally the MCR platform, Author's note.).

Ripley on 1 September 1858 (as will be recounted later).

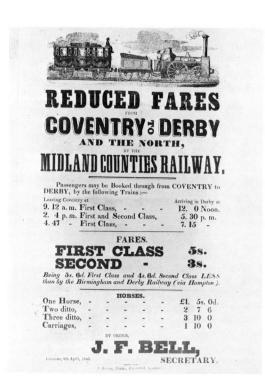

A railway route involving Derby and Holyhead had been planned as early as November 1845 by the Derby, Uttoxeter and Stafford Railway but the scheme was abandoned on 10 March 1846. Ultimately there emerged the Stafford & Uttoxeter Railway, opened on 23 December 1867 to be worked by the GNR.

The only other company to begin railway operations in the county before 1850 which involved Derby was the North Staffordshire Railway with headquarters at Stoke-on-Trent.

The first NSR line in the area opened between Uttoxeter and Burton-upon-Trent on 11 September 1848 with a later branch to Willington, where it joined the Midland (ex-B&DJR) main line, opening on 13 July, 1849. Since the main line between Uttoxeter and Stoke had opened for both passenger and goods traffic on 7 August 1848 and the section of line from Stoke westwards to join the L&NWR at Crewe on 9 October 1848, a through route was established for traffic from Derby to the northwest, and later to North Wales with the opening of the Chester to Holyhead line in 1850.

Above:
Reduced fares leaflet of the MCR during the ruinous period of competition with the B&DJR, dated April 1843. *Author's Collection*

Below:
The Midland Hotel, Derby, about 1899.
MR Official, Crown Copyright courtesy the National Railway Museum

Above:
The refurbished NMR houses in Calvert Street (formerly North Street). *Author*

Arrangements were made with the MR for the NSR Co to use Derby station, as minuted by the Midland Board on 4 July 1849, but which required that the NSR meet all Parliamentary charges and pay for the use of the MR's pilot engines, empty wagons, trucks and carriages at 1s per mile per engine and 2d per carriage per mile. A charge of £2,000 per annum was to be paid for the use of Derby station facilities, the engine house, supply of water, use of the coke stage and for the services of clerks, porters and other servants.

A penalty of one shilling was to be levied for every horse box, wagon, truck or vehicle above 30 in number remaining in Derby or on the line to Willington Junction over 24hr and 2s 6d for every engine above three in number in the same period.

The MR would control the junction and the NSR were to pay for the 'junction works, signals, repairs, watching, lighting and alterations'.

At the Burton end a further £500 per annum was to be paid for the use of the line between the station and Burton Junction and the use of the engine house, coke stage and supply of water, etc.

As previously mentioned, Derby was already linked to London (Euston) via the L&BR but on 18 June 1844 at 5.03am, George Stephenson was one of a group of passengers who left that station on a train bound for the far north.

Diverting at Rugby Junction on to the former MCR the train ran via Leicester and Derby and thence by the former NMR through Normanton and via the Y&NMR to York and on to Gateshead, using a newly completed part of the N&DJ line, arriving there at 2.35pm having covered the 303 miles in 9hr 32min at the incredible average speed, including stops to change engines, of almost 32mph. The days of the main line railway had arrived and, just as Hudson and others had foreseen, Derby had become an important interchange and conjunction of several through routes.

Development of goods traffic was clearly to the forefront of the Directors thinking when on 5 March 1845 they appointed Mr West as first Manager of the Midland Goods Department at a salary of £300 per year, his brief being 'to obtain goods traffic for the line and to suggest any measures for the better effecting of the same' and also to be 'constantly on the alert visiting the stations and the various towns to hunt up goods traffic from all practicable sources'. As we shall see, it was to be some years before the traffic potential of Derby itself was satisfactorily tapped by the MR.

Developments in the station area in the first

Above:
The MR Institute which opened in February 1894. *MR Official, Author's Collection*

years of the MR included the erection of a gas house by Gascoyne & Son of Derby for £275 which was agreed on 26 November 1844; conversion of part of the old MCR engine house into stables early in 1845 at 'a cost of about £60' and the removal and transfer of the old B&DJR goods shed to Wilnecote, which was ordered on 11 February 1845.

Derby can take pride in being one of the first places where the idea of a station hotel was adopted, for the original plans of 1839 show an 'L' shaped building on the same site as that now occupied by the Midland Hotel. Unfortunately, exact details of its construction have not been unearthed but a minute of the NMR Co meeting at Derby on 17 December 1839 recorded that Mr Jackson's offer to erect an hotel adjoining Derby station was accepted. This was the same Thomas Jackson who had been responsible for building Derby station and whose firm was based at Pimlico, London. According to subsequent newspaper reports he constructed the hotel from his own resources as a commercial enterprise, but at his bankruptcy hearing, recorded in the *Derby Mercury* of 2 November 1859, when his debts exceeded £300,000, it was reported that although he was the owner of the hotel, it was subject to a mortgage and could not therefore be sold, although 'the value of the furniture, silver plate, horses and wine cellar stocks' was put at £5,000.

On 14 August 1860, the MR directors discussed the necessity of having good hotels at their principal stations and since the Midland Hotel had been offered for sale, it was purchased from the then owner Mrs Julia Ann

Blunt and others through Alphaeus H. Robotham, on behalf of the MR, for £10,050 and was later transferred to the MR Co by an indenture dated 1 March 1862.

Her Majesty, Queen Victoria, paid a visit to Derby and stayed in the hotel in September 1849. E. C. Cuff was then the Manager and he was followed by Mrs Susan Chatfield. The tariff of charges circa 1858 were as follows: Bed, single — 2s; breakfast, meat and eggs — 2s; breakfast, hot meal — 2s 6d; dinners 2s 6d and upwards; plain tea 1s 6d; sitting rooms 3s, 4s and 5s; wax lights 1s and 1s 6d; fires 1s and 1s 6d; attendance 1s; and 'the usual charges for commercial gentlemen'.

To complete the hotel's history, additional wings were added during Mr Plock's time as Manager in 1873 at a cost of £3,200 and again in 1884. In 1877 the MR obtained an Act to work the hotel as a part of their railway undertaking. In the 1930s the hotel was further enlarged to provide additional bedrooms and bathrooms, extension of the dining rooms and the addition of a lounge between the two wings. Central heating, hot and cold running water in 50 bedrooms and three new bathrooms were installed at a total cost of some £9,400.

Since then additional private bathrooms have been added and in April 1982 the hotel was sold by British Transport Hotels, a subsidiary of British Rail, to the private Midland Hotels Ltd who made an outlay of some £150,000 on its renovation and restoration to something approaching its original style with long, sweeping arches, white walls with gold detail and tropical palms. It is still a first class hotel and also a popular place for luncheons, dinners and conferences.

In the area adjacent to the station, and on the opposite side of Railway Terrace built originally to link the station with Siddals Lane, a small housing estate was erected by Thomas Jackson and possibly also designed by Francis Thompson. The dwellings were built in a triangular block, the three sides comprising *North* Street, *Midland* Place and *Railway* Terrace, thus forming the name of the NMR. The houses were paid for by that company and erected in 1841-43, totalling 80 in number plus the Brunswick Inn at the northern apex of the triangle adjacent to Siddals Lane end with a shop next to it in North Street whilst the other two apexes were also occupied by shops. The most imposing houses with stone dressed doorways and a parapet hiding the roofs and fronting on to Railway Terrace, were those occupied by railway officers, foremen and senior staff, some of whom were 'on call' by a

Above:
The Brunswick Inn, a favourite meeting place for railwaymen, before its recent renovation.
Author

bell installed in their houses, whilst the terraced dwellings behind in two cul-de-sacs and in North Street were of much simpler construction for other workers. A further 12 houses were built beyond the triangle on the north side of North Street.

Within this housing complex a rope walk formerly ran along the back gardens in North Street (later Calvert Street). It was in existence in 1852 but there appears to be no record of when it ceased producing ropes, although it was certainly out of use by 1882.

Part of this complex is now occupied by the Railway Institute building opened by George Ernest Paget, Chairman of the MR Board of Directors, on 16 February 1894. This occupies a site at the corner of Railway Terrace and Midland Place formerly occupied by eight houses in the former and four in the latter and in addition, four houses in the Leeds Place cul-de-sac were demolished to accommodate the new building.

The Institute owes its origin to a group of MR employees who, in December 1850, began meeting in the Brunswick Inn and who formed a Reading Society. A few weeks later they decided to establish a reading room and subscription library and, following a petition signed by 423 employees, which was presented to the MR's directors on 14 February 1851

asking for the use of a room, two cottages were provided in Leeds Place for this purpose for the use of the 'Derby Railway Literary Institution'. They were offered two rooms below the new Shareholders' room in 1857 and eventually moved into their new palatial red brick premises at the present Institute in 1894.

Membership of the Institute was open to all employees on payment of a small weekly subscription and facilities included a large library to house the then stock of over 14,000 volumes, a magazine and newspaper room, a waiting room, three classrooms, a lecture and concert hall to seat 500, chess, card and billiard rooms and a coffee room.

The library operated a lending service over the entire MR system, staff at stations and depots, selecting from the catalogue a choice of books which would then be sent by passenger train for the loan period and returned afterwards in special small containers. The library was eventually closed in 1963 and its collection sold except for the railway reference section which has passed into the care of the Midland Railway Trust at the Midland Railway Centre, Butterley, Derbyshire. The Institute is now a British Railways Staff Association Branch, No 105, and has been re-modelled on social club lines.

Mention should also be made of the conversion of four houses, Nos 1-4 Leeds Place, to accommodate the MR's ticket printing office which was demolished during renovation and restoration work in the estate in 1982.

The Brunswick Inn, mentioned above, opened its doors in 1843 and the then proprietor Mr Harvey Lane advertised that the house was 'now open for the reception of families and commercial gentlemen, no expense having been spared to render every appointment in the establishment both comfortable and convenient.

Terms:
Breakfast, plain		1s 6d
Ditto, with meat etc		2s 0d
Dinner		2s 0d
Tea		1s 6d
Supper		1s 6d
Beds		2s 0d
Wine (per bottle)		5s 0d

Horses and carriages let to hire'.

In later years the inn was a favourite resort of railwaymen of all grades and has recently been renovated, along with the remaining railway houses, due to the efforts of the Derby Civic Society and the Derbyshire Historic Buildings Trust which has saved this important area from a demolition and clearance scheme for an intended new road.

Returning briefly to the housing situation — within a few years housing developments took place beyond the original NMR 'estate'. Nelson Street, Hulland Street, Carrington Street and Park Street all provided accommodation for the growing staff of the MR and soon new streets beyond the London Road were developed, Oxford Street, Regent Street and even the Osmaston Road containing the residence of a person in charge of an office or other staff with a salary of £150 per annum.

Eventually staff were living around and beyond the Arboretum, the first public park in England opened on 16 September 1840, in the Rose Hill, Pear Tree and Normanton districts, and in due course came tramways, cycles and then buses and in modern times motor cycles and private cars, affording an opportunity for workers to live even further afield in healthier districts yet still be able to travel to work in a convenient time.

Adjacent to St Andrew's Goods Wharf once stood Derby's railwaymen's Church of the same name. It provided not only spiritual but physical welfare and schooling for the children of railwaymen in a day school opened in September 1863. A nursery was also provided and free evening classes were held to enable adults to learn the three R's: reading, writing and arithmetic.

Midland shareholders were pressed to contribute to the church's construction fund, launched by Michael Bass, the MP for Derby, funds being raised on condition that every sitting should be free.

Designed by Sir George Gilbert Scott, architect of St Pancras station, the Church was consecrated by the Bishop of Lichfield on Ascension Day 1866 but was not completed for a further 25 years when the spire was added.

It was finally declared redundant, the body of the church having been demolished by March 1970 although the spire proved more obstinate, not being finally cleared away for several months afterwards. The site is now occupied by Government offices.

Below:
St Andrew's, the railwaymen's church which was situated on the London Road and which was demolished in 1969-70.
Derby Evening Telegraph *courtesy Derby Libraries*

The Midland Locomotive and Carriage & Wagon Works and Motive Power Depot (1840-1947)

The repair and manufacturing facilities for the three railway companies, whose lines met at Derby, were originally quite separate.

The site chosen in two cases was to the south-east of the station, but thousands of tons of earth and gravel had to be tipped into a low-lying area of land, adjacent to the River Derwent, purchased from landowner Mr J. C. B. Burrough of Chetwynd Park, Shropshire, on 12 November 1838, before building work could commence. The level of the major part of the site was raised by some 8ft and only the goods wharves of all three companies, situated alongside the Derby Canal, remained at the lower level, now known as the 'bottom yard'.

Twelve months later the workshops and offices for the NMR Co, like the station to the designs of Francis Thompson, were ready for occupation. The central feature was an engine roundhouse, polygonal in shape and with 16 sides from each of which a line of rails capable of accommodating two locomotives, ran towards the central turntable. The roundhouse

had a lantern-topped pointed roof 48ft 10in high comprising a 7ft 10in high lantern atop a 23ft high roof supported on 18ft high cast-iron columns. The slate roof was laid on wooden boards.

Below:

Plan of Derby Works showing different stages of development. 1 Old Engine Sheds 1, 2 and 3; **2** Paint Shop; **3** Tool Shop; **4** Brass Fitting Shop; **5** Tool Room; **6** Grinding Shop; **7** Tool and Fitting Shop; **8** Erecting Shop; **9** Offices (later Met Lab); **10** Brass Foundry; **11** Coppersmiths; **12** Electric Shop (former Erecting Shop); **13** Tender Shop (former Erecting Shop); **14** Pattern Shop (former Paint Shop); **15** Lagging Shop (former Tender Shop); **16** Loco Stores (former NM Engine Shop); **17** Main Offices; **18** Millwrights (former NM Carriage Shop); **19** General Stores (former MC Engine Shop, Machine Shop and Shed); **20** Works Canteen; **21** Boiler Shop; **22** Wheel and Tyre Shop; **23** Turning Shop; **24** Press Shop; **25** Wheel Turning Shop; **26** Forge; **27** Concentration Depot; **28** Iron Foundry; **29** Chair Foundry; **30** Smith Shop; **31** Power Station; **32** Saw Mill and Timber Yard.

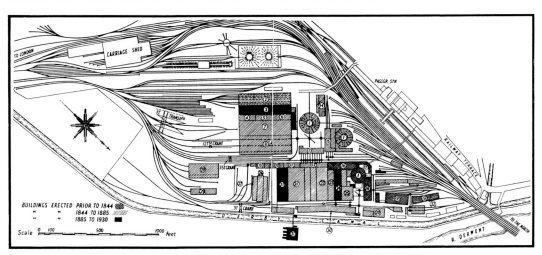

Above:
View inside the old No 2 erecting shop, probably taken about 1888. The building later became the electric shop. *MR Official, Author's Collection*

The two main workshops formed oblique wings and, as viewed from the station, that to the right was the engine workshop 184ft 6in long and 70ft 6in wide with a roof supported by 20 massive cast-iron columns, whilst to the left were the carriage workshops (now the millwrights shop) 191ft 6in long and also 70ft 6in wide. Total cost of this accommodation was £62,000. The original single storey offices fronting the central area had a second floor added in 1859-60 with a third floor in 1893.

Housed in the central clocktower is the original North Midland clock made by Derby's John Whitehurst the younger, in 1840, and still going strong, 145 years later. The dials were originally at a lower level but with the addition of the third storey of office accommodation in 1893 a new set of drive rods were made by John Smith & Sons of Derby (successors to Whitehurst) to connect the clock mechanism to the new dial room above the bell chamber which houses the old bell from St Pancras chapel in London which had been demolished to permit the MR line into its new station there.

The MCR Co established their workshops at the north end of the station on a site immediately adjacent to the NMR Shops. Accommodation here comprised an engine

shed 134ft long and 52ft wide and an engine workshop and machine shop 200ft long×93ft wide with a repair shop 93ft×85ft attached, all of which were substantially built in brick. A large water tank 48ft 6in long and 27ft wide gave an adequate supply for all three companies' requirements.

The B&DJR's main headquarters and workshops were at Hampton-in-Arden and the only accommodation at Derby was a brick engine shed 150ft long and 48ft wide, built by T. & W. Cooper at a cost of some £4,000 and situated at the south end of the station near to where the London Road bridge crossed over the B&DJR main line.

Some figures are available from NMR records for the six months from January to June 1842. 73 miles of track were being worked by 16 engines in steam daily, except Sundays, out of a total stock of 40. 5,694 miles were run by passenger trains, 4,925 on goods trains and 938 by 'assistant and pilot trains'. The Locomotive Department staff was 197, mostly located at Derby and the total weekly wages bill was £261/13s/10d. Robert Stephenson had

Above:
Inside No 1 shed, the oldest roundhouse in the world still in regular use, as it appeared in 1905. It is now used for the repair of breakdown cranes. *MR Official, Author's Collection*

been the Manager of Motive Power from February 1839 until August 1842 but there was also a Superintendent of the Locomotive Department, this post being filled by William Prime Marshall at a salary of £200 per annum until 4 April 1843 when he resigned and was replaced by Thomas Kirtley as Locomotive & Carriage Superintendent at a salary of £250 per annum.

With the amalgamation of the three companies to form the new Midland Railway Co as from 10 May 1844 Thomas Kirtley found himself in contention with his younger brother, Matthew and Josiah Kearsley of the MCR for the post of Locomotive and Carriage & Wagon Superintendent with the new company. Somewhat surprisingly, and possibly on account of strong representations by George and Robert Stephenson, it was Matthew who was offered the post at a salary of £250 per annum, a full £50 more than his B&DJR salary at the age of only 31.

He immediately began to bring order and standardisation to the wide variety of motive power inherited from the old companies, some 90 or so locomotives in all. Many were already too light for the weight of trains then running and Matthew came out in favour of six-wheeled locomotives. He took note of the time out of use awaiting spares from private

manufacturers for many of the engines and accordingly developed the workshops at Derby not only to repair old locomotives but to build new.

In September 1851 number 147, a six-wheel-coupled inside frames 0-6-0 goods tender engine emerged from the shops followed by three more and in December 1851 the first new 2-2-2 passenger engine number 96, went into traffic, a Derby version of E. B. Wilson's 'Jenny Lind' type.

By 1855 Kirtley was able to report that 33 new engines in all had been completed by the Derby shops which were also not only repairing and re-building other engines, and in the same complex repairing, maintaining and re-painting all the rolling stock in addition to constructing new passenger carriages and goods wagons of all kinds, although, as in the locomotive field, batches of new stock were still being purchased from private builders, albeit now to Midland specification and standards.

Above:
The coppersmiths shop in Derby Locomotive Works as it was on 14 May 1917.
MR Official, Author's Collection

Below:
Kirtley '70' class 2-4-0 number 76, built at Derby in October 1863. *MR Official, Author's Collection*

New extensions to the workshop accommodation included a Wheel shop, a Repair and Painting shop in 1856 at a cost of £7,500 and a Brass Foundry and Mess Room at a cost of £2,500 in 1859. A footbridge across the running lines from the station to the clock tower was added in 1860 at a cost of £1,000.

Although a second roundhouse had been completed in mid-February 1847 to house a further 16 locomotives, a third was soon found to be necessary and added in 1852, being larger than Nos 1 and 2 and having 24 roads, four having access from outside. This new roundhouse, 170ft in diameter with a 90ft diameter clear area in the centre and a total height to the top of the lantern roof of 51ft 6in, was designed by the MR's architect, John H. Sanders, and built by George Thompson at a cost of around £6,500. A further mess room was added in 1862 and in the following year a

new Saw Shed and Tinsmiths and Coppersmiths shops.

By this time the workshops area had increased four-fold and the staff now numbered over 2,000. In 1864 a new Millwrights shop and a new Carriage shop were erected and the following year travelling cranes were provided for these and a new Smiths shop built on the bottom yard.

Returning to locomotive construction — Kirtley moved, with his 0-6-0 goods engines, to the straight-framed type commencing with number 187 completed in June 1857 this design being used for many years whilst, in addition to his double-framed 2-2-2s for passenger work, the first 2-4-0 goods engine appeared from Derby in September 1856. It was not until June 1859 that number 150, a 2-4-0 designed specifically for passenger work with 6ft diameter driving wheels and 16in diameter × 22in stroke cylinders emerged from the works, the first of a long-lived type which survived many 'renewal and re-building' operations.

In 1863 Kirtley introduced the curved framed 0-6-0 as the new standard goods engine commencing with number 246 in December and also produced three types of 2-4-0 express passenger engine, the '80', '70' and '50' classes. The '80' class were built to work trains to King's Cross (St Pancras the MR's own terminus in London not then open) and for excursion traffic and special trains run in connection with the Great Exhibition of 1862. The '70' class, consisting of two sub-groups, was used on the lighter express trains and the '50' class mainly on services to Birmingham and the West. Kirtley also indulged in both re-building and new building to create a fleet of 0-6-0WT locomotive which were used for a variety of branch line and shunting duties, two being built specifically to bank trains up the Lickey incline south of Birmingham.

In September 1866 No 156, the first of a new class of 2-4-0 tender engines, emerged from the works followed by 22 more and five further sets of frames were cut, but the engines not actually built during Kirtley's lifetime. These engines had frames cut from solid plate, replacing the old type which had separate tie bars to the horns, 6ft 2in diameter driving wheels and 16½in diameter×22in stroke cylinders and were put to use on the fastest express passenger trains. They were followed by the renowned '800' class of 2-4-0 of which 12 were built at Derby between February and July, 1870 with a further 30 by Neilson & Co Ltd of Glasgow.

The Derby engines were allocated to Leicester and the Neilsons to Kentish Town (12), Leeds (8) and Bristol (10) and were later re-built by Johnson to work traffic over the new Settle & Carlisle line in 1876.

Other classes, including the '890' class and the '96' class, completed Kirtley's Derby-built fleet of 2-4-0s for passenger traffic whilst, apart from some 0-4-4WTs for Metropolitan traffic, the ubiquitous 0-6-0 goods tender engine fulfilled the remainder of motive power requirements.

Kirtley was also responsible for carriage and wagon affairs and the repair, alteration and new building of stock took place in the Derby workshops. Four months workload during 1849 included the construction of three new second class carriages, one replacement enclosed third class carriage, 12 new goods wagons with spring buffers and three replacement goods wagons whilst repair work included 18 first class carriages, six composite, 21 second class carriages, seven third class carriages, one post office carriage, 42 guards vans, six horse boxes, two carriage trucks, 414 wagons and the painting of 184 wagons. The weekly wagon bill for the same period was £1,449, the cost of repairing

Above:
Kirtley '800' class 2-4-0 No 64, built at Derby in May 1870 and fitted with a Westinghouse pump for working air-braked trains to the north.
MR Official, Author's Collection

Below:
Kirtley 20ft 1st class carriage number 101 built at Derby about 1865. *MR Official, Author's Collection*

engines £419/2s/6d and repairing carriages £204/8s/2d.

Carriage & Wagon re-organisation

In the period up to 1873, when the MR directors decided that conditions on the original works site were too cramped and a new carriage and wagon works needed to be created on a separate site under a separate Carriage & Wagon Superintendent, the old works built a large quantity of stock including 1st, 2nd and 3rd class four-wheeled carriages, composites, family saloons, carriage trucks, an officer's inspecting saloon, milk vans, poultry trucks and a large variety of cattle and goods vehicles and brake vans in addition to much re-building and conversion work and ordinary repair work. More than 1,400 carriages were

Above:
Pullman drawing room car number 8, built as 'Albion' and put into traffic on 9 October 1876. The photograph clearly shows the ornate lining with which the car was decorated.
MR Official, Author's Collection

Below:
Clayton clerestory bogie 3rd-class brake number 323 built at Derby in 1878.
MR Official, courtesy Midland Railway Trust Ltd

either built or renewed between 1858 and 1873 of which 264 were additions to capital stock.

Matthew Kirtley had a large part in the plans for re-organising the Locomotive Works facilities, first discussed in 1870, and had already agreed on 4 March that a separate Carriage & Wagon Superintendent should be appointed. However, his untimely death on 24 May 1873 at the age of 60 left the MR directors with not one but two posts to fill.

On the Locomotive side the company was most fortunate in securing the services of Samuel Waite Johnson, who had been Locomotive and Carriage & Wagon Superintendent of the Great Eastern Railway at Stratford since 1866. He took office as Locomotive Superintendent on 1 July 1873, at a salary of £2,000 per annum, on the same day as the new Carriage & Wagon Superintendent, Thomas Gething Clayton took up his post at £700 per annum. Clayton came from the Great Western Railway at Swindon, where in 1868 he had superintended the erection of the company's new shops, and was selected from 41 applicants.

Clayton set to work to reorganise and modernise the MR's carriage stock, most of which was archaic. Four-wheelers with roof rails were still in extensive use, there being at that time no bogie vehicles, but as a result of Alport's visit to America, 1873 saw the importing from Detroit of kits of parts for the first bogie Pullman cars for assembly in new

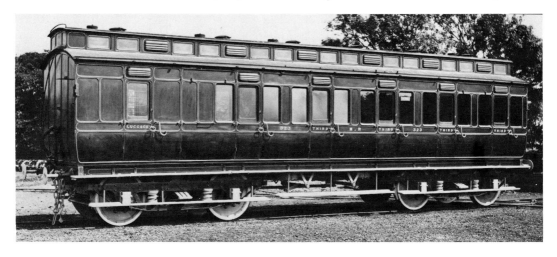

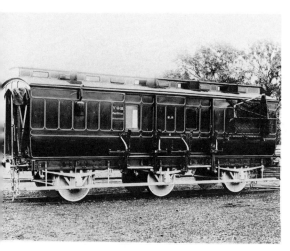

Above:
Midland 30ft post-office tender No 6 built at Derby in 1879 as a carriage for sorting letters etc.
MR Official, courtesy Midland Railway Trust Ltd

Below:
Clayton six-wheeled bogie composite No 481, built at Derby in 1886, on No 3 steam traverser in the carriage works.
MR Official, Author's Collection

A 50 acre area of land was purchased in November 1873 and reserved for the erection of the new works and Clayton's block plan was approved on 2 December. Detailed plans received the approval of the General Purposes Committee the following January and on 31 March 1874 the Way & Works Committee was instructed to proceed at once with the erection of a Saw Mill, Machine and Fitting shop, Smithy, Stores and Foundry. Plans for new offices were approved on 30 June and on 16 March 1875 instructions were issued for the erection of a new Wagon Shop, Carriage building and Carriage painting Shops.

By February 1877 Clayton was able to report that machines were being moved from the old works to the new and that carriage repairs had begun, although at his request the Etches Park sheds remained in use for storing freshly painted carriages. Two new bogie carriages had already been turned out from these shops the previous year and were the first signs of a major revolution in MR carriage design.

By 1878 some 13½ acres were covered by Workshops at a total cost of some £300,000 and were in full production by the year's end. Among the first deliveries were 40ft bogie carriages, 26ft 3rd class brakes, 40ft family carriages and some 30ft carriages for Post Office use. The first 54ft bogie vehicles to be built at Derby were for the Midland, Scottish Joint stock services between St Pancras, Edinburgh Waverley and Glasgow St Enoch, 10 being completed by June 1879 at a cost of £915 each. These were followed in 1883 by the first 54ft vehicles for the MR's own London-Liverpool services and some four years later a mixed batch of four different sleeping cars was constructed for trial to determine which of the types should replace the Pullman

separate shops built alongside the main line to London on its south side. These cars entered service on 1 June 1874 following successful trials the previous March.

A new carriage repair and paint shed had been erected at Etches Park in 1864 at the extreme south west corner of the company's land for use as repair shops and a new paint shop opened there in 1873 for temporary use until the new buildings of the Carriage & Wagon Works were ready.

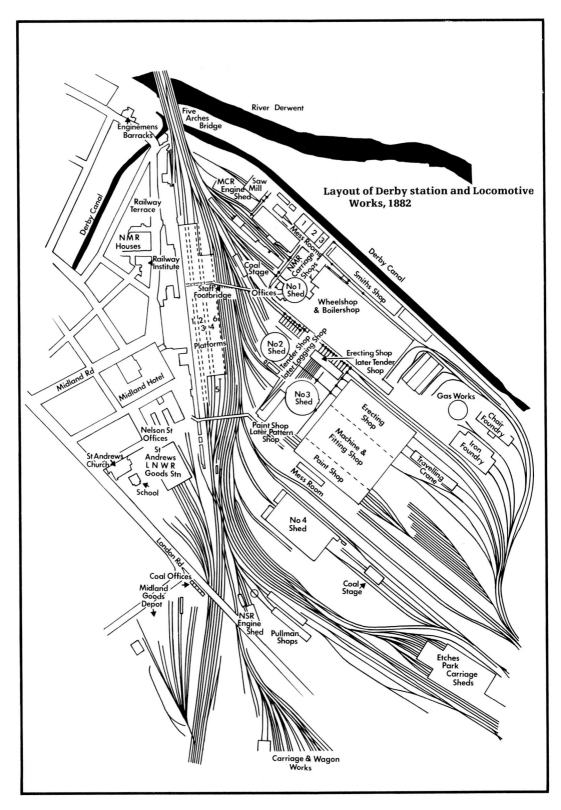

Layout of Derby station and Locomotive Works, 1882

River Derwent

Five Arches Bridge

Enginemens Barracks

Derby Canal

Railway Terrace

NMR Houses

Railway Institute

MCR Engine Shed

Saw Mill

Mess Rooms 1 2 3

Coal Stage

NMR Carriage Shops

Offices

No 1 Shed

Smiths Shop

Derby Canal

Staff Footbridge

1 2 6 3 4

Platforms

Wheelshop & Boilershop

No 2 Shed

Tender Shop later Logging Shop

Erecting Shop later Tender Shop

Midland Rd

Midland Hotel

5

No 3 Shed

Erecting Shop

Gas Works

Chair Foundry

Nelson St Offices

Paint Shop Later Pattern Shop

Machine & Fitting Shop

Iron Foundry

St Andrews Church

St Andrews L N W R Goods Stn

School

Paint Shop

Mess Room

Travelling Crane

No 4 Shed

London Rd

Coal Offices

Midland Goods Depot

NSR Engine Shed

Pullman Shops

Coal Stage

Etches Park Carriage Sheds

Carriage & Wagon Works

28

Sleeping Cars, although in fact four further new cars were ordered from that company in 1899.

Large quantities of goods vehicles were also being turned out including goods brake vans, cattle wagons, timber trucks and coke wagons and no less than 1,000 each of both high and low sided goods wagons. A special shop had been erected in 1882 and dedicated to repairing and modifying the large fleet of private owner wagons bought in by the MR because of their unsound design and poor maintenance and up to 1895 no less than 66,813 wagons were purchased at a fair valuation from their owners and put into safe working order.

In July, 1888 the MR completed the purchase of the entire Osmaston Park Estate comprising some 235 acres from Sir R. R. Wilmot and the trustees of Sir George Wilmot-Horton, to be used for further extension of the workshops area, and included was Osmaston Hall itself, later used for headquarters purposes.

Above left:
Part of the paint shop, now known as 'G' shop, as it appeared in c1890 with a variety of stock being painted. *MR Official, Author's Collection*

Above right:
The carriage repair shop, now 'C' shop, as it appeared about 1890 showing the hydraulic lifting gear for removing carriage bodies from their bogies. *MR Official, Author's Collection*

Plan of Derby Carriage & Wagon Works, 1910.
1 Messrooms; **2** Carriage Repairing and Lifting Shops; **3** Panel shed; **4** Finishing; **5** Carriage Repairing Shop; **6** Carriage Building Shop; **7** Wagon Building Shop; **8** Sawmill; **9** Timber Bending; **10** Timber Drying Shed; **11** Offices; **12** Hair Carding Shop; **13** Trimming Shop; **14** Carriage Painting Shop; **15** Carriage Painting and Varnishing Shop; **16** Carriage Lifting, Wagon Lifting and Steel Frame Building; **17** Fitting Shop, Machine Shop and Wheel Lathes; **18** Smithy, Spring making; **19** Brassworkers; **20** Iron Stores; **21** Iron Foundry; **22** Stores; **23** Brass Foundry; **24** Smithy, Forge; **25** Drop Stamping Shop; **26** Wheel Shop; **27** Breaking Up; **28** Coal Wagon Repairing Shop.

Plan of Carriage & Wagon Works
MIDLAND RAILWAY
DERBY 1910

Locomotive Developments

Following his arrival at the Locomotive Works Samuel Johnson put in hand the construction of a number of new locomotives including 0-4-4 passenger tank engines for suburban and branch passenger services, 0-6-0T engines and his new design of 0-6-0 based on the Sharp Stewart 0-6-0s purchased by him for the Great Eastern. On the passenger locomotive side Johnson followed up the Kirtley '890' class 2-4-0 with further locomotives incorporating his own improvements and 2-4-0s continued to be built at Derby up to 1881. In September, 1882 the first Derby built Johnson 4-4-0, No 1562, appeared having 6ft 8½in diameter driving wheels and 18in diameter×26in stroke cylinders. These followed the first batches built outside by Kitson & Co and Dubs from 1876 onwards.

The first of Johnson's beautiful 4-2-2 'Spinner' passenger locomotives, No 25, emerged from the works in June, 1887

forerunner of 95 such engines turned out over the next 14 years and which, to many, were the epitome of good mechanical design coupled with graceful appearance. They were economical engines consuming only 20-21lb of coal per mile with their average load of 115 tons, for their main use was hauling the light, fast express trains, on occasions reaching 90mph. One, No 2601 *Princess of Wales*, with her 7ft 9½in diameter driving wheels and 19½in diameter×26in cylinders with piston valves, swept the board at the Paris Exhibition of 1900 where it was awarded the Grand Prix.

Above:
Johnson 0-6-0T No 1413 completed at Derby in June 1880.
MR Official, courtesy Midland Railway Trust Ltd

Below:
Johnson 4-4-0 No 1666 built at Derby and put into traffic in November 1883.
MR Official, Author's Collection

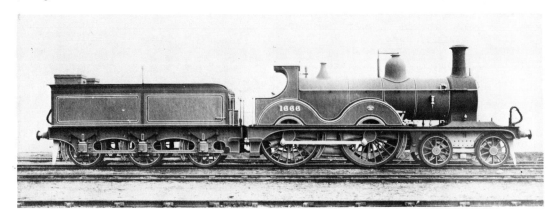

On the motive power depot scene the three
previous roundhouses at Derby have already
been mentioned, but the one known as '4 shed',
quite simply because it was the fourth such
building provided, and the one remembered
most vividly from the recent past, was the first
of two intended sheds, No 5 never in fact being
erected.

Johnson had reported to the Locomotive
Committee on 28 February, 1888 that he had
now 99 engines regularly in steam at Derby
and that all the engines leaving the Derby
shops had also to be accommodated during
trials and for these No 2 Shed held only 16 and
No 3 Shed 24. Plans were therefore got out for a
48 engine twin turntable shed with associated
sidings to be built on land between the Works
and the main line to London, formerly
occupied by wagon sidings. The original plan
showed the two twin-turntable sheds of
rectangular shape positioned adjacent to each
other, but offset end to end. Messrs William
Walkerdine of Derby were the builders of the
first shed which cost £29,800 and incorporated
twin 50ft turntables built by Messrs Cowans
Sheldon at a cost of £640 each, 22 stabling
roads leading from each table. It was brought
into use early in 1890, but the second shed was
never built and instead a 60ft turntable
costing £1,065 and supplied by Messrs Eastwood Swingler & Co, was installed on the site.

It had 16 radiating lines and was brought into
use in 1900-1.

At the same time an extensive system of
carriage sidings, with a carriage shed, and
costing £33,770 was erected at Chaddesden
sidings, approval being given on 2 June 1899.
This was in addition to carriage sheds at
Etches Park which were erected concurrently
with the development of No 4 shed. Etches
Park incidentally is named after William
Jeffrey Etches, a prosperous cheese factor of
the town whose warehouse once occupied part
of the north end of Platform 1, and whose
rather unpretentious house was surrounded
by the garden or 'park' which contained
statuary removed to the Derby Arboretum
after the property was acquired by the MR.

Above:
A night-time view in No 4 shed at Derby taken by the then new gas lighting on 10 March 1910.
MR Official, Author's Collection

Left:
Derby 4 shed mechanical coaling plant on 10 March 1936 with LMS compound 4-4-0 No 1123 taking on supplies.
LMS Official, Author's Collection

Derby was appropriately MR Shed No 1 with an allocation of 112 engines in 1880 and more than 120 engines in 1892 the latter including no less than 82 Kirtley double-framed 0-6-0s (nine more than in 1880). By 1914 the passenger fleet had been increased by almost 20 Class 2P 4-4-0s and 30 Class 3P 'Belpaire' 4-4-0s along with nine Johnson 4-2-2s.

The shed became 17A under the 1935 LMS Re-organisation of Motive Power and still had over 100 locomotives increasing to almost 140 in the 1950s. A mechanical coaling plant was erected by Henry Lees & Co and two steel framed ash plants erected by Babcock & Wilcox Ltd, all in 1936 when the old hand coaling stage passed out of use.

Following dieselisation in the early 1960s when BR/Sulzer 'Peaks' had displaced 'Jubilee' and Class 5 4-6-0s, Derby was demoted to a sub shed, coded 16C in September 1963 as part of the Toton district and the shed closed to steam on 6 March 1967. The large '4 shed' itself was demolished in 1967 leaving only the old offices as a signing-on point together with stores and messroom at the station end of the site. Now only the historic No 1 roundhouse of 1840 remains as a Crane Repair shop.

One particular character shines from the pages of Pratt's writings in connection with the engine shed and this was a foreman cleaner, a rough and ignorant bully who rejoiced in the name 'Bumblefoot'. Many drivers looked back on their days as cleaners under his jurisdiction with painful memories — the work being dirty, hard, inadequately paid and they were obliged to work until four o'clock on Saturday afternoons. Bumble was a master of the malapropism; on one occasion addressing cleaners on an engine 'how many on ya are there up theer' and upon receiving the answer 'three' replied 'then hafe on you cum down here!' His advice to a miscreant about to go up before the Divisional Super-intendent was 'Dunna yo, answer no questions as they dunna axe yer. Keep yer tongue on terra firma' and a parting shot to members of a cleaning gang was once 'I've towd yer all I know, an' now yer know nowt!' One day, however, he got his 'cum-uppance' being caught stealing a small piece of fireclay and as if by magic a set of doggerel verses was passed round about the offence, although the worst of all was to see the words 'Bumblefoot-Fireclay' in huge white letters around the cupalo on the inside of the shed!

Returning to Locomotive Works matters, a new entrance was provided from 9 January 1899 with the opening of the Hulland Street entrance with a footbridge spanning the lines at the south end of the station and leading down a ramp opposite the north end of the paint shop. This entrance had been under discussion since December 1883 when a request was made for a subway passing beneath the tracks. Nothing was done until a memorandum from 1,003 workmen was received in July 1891 asking for an additional road entrance to be made.

Eventually an estimate of £7,862 was accepted when a saving of £3,210 per annum was identified through men getting more quickly to work and avoiding the necessity of a new messroom plus further savings made in getting stores and parcels into the works. Approval was given on 17 September, 1896 by the General Purposes Committee and the tender of Sir W. G. A. Armstrong Whitworth to supply a hydraulic lift at each end of the footbridge at a total cost of £600 was also

Above:
The mess room at Derby No 4 shed on 7 March 1910 with the mid-day meal 'snap' baskets laid out in readiness, each with its owner's sandwiches, meat pie or other filling eatable delight. *MR Official, Author's Collection*

Below:
Lowering cores into a cylinder mould in the Derby Locomotive Works iron foundry on 7 March 1910. *MR Official, Author's Collection*

accepted. This footbridge is now closed and at the time of writing awaited demolition.

During construction of this new entrance the old NSR 'Cosy Corner' had to be demolished. Here old John Faulkner had held a harbour of refuge for the privileged few in a room that was 'like a bar with no drinks and a barber's shop with no barber'. John, a temperance

Above:
Deeley '990' class 4-4-0 No 993, built at Derby in June 1909, taking on water beside No 4 shed coaling plant, one of typical later Midland design. *MR Official, Author's Collection*

Below:
Attractive Deeley 0-4-0T engine completed at Derby in August 1907 and built for light shunting duties.
MR Official courtesy Midland Railway Trust Ltd

figure, offered homely advice to all and one of his regulars was William Burdett, the last of Derby's coach drivers who finished his days driving the omnibus to and from Derby Market Place. Sad to relate, during construction of the new entrance, old John took a chill and died and thus another small piece of tradition passed into history.

At the same period agreement was reached in July 1887 for a new road to be made into the Locomotive Works for workmen residing at Osmaston, Alvaston and Newtown. As a result of a petition signed by 138 workmen affected, the road, a gatehouse and a fenced cinder path 6ft wide and lit by 10 gas lamps were provided in 1888 from the end of Deadmans Lane into the works.

Johnson's final fling was the introduction of his compound 4-4-0 express passenger locomotives, numbered 2631-5, the first of which commenced work on 26 November 1901. These had one 19in×26in high pressure cylinder between the frames and two 21in×26in low pressure cylinders outside the frames. Although at first christened an 'ugly brute', No 2631 and its sisters soon proved their abilities and, with modifications, Johnson's successor Richard Deeley continued to build them adding a further 40 and they were also adopted by the LMS as a standard design with the building of a further 195 between 1924 and 1932. They were the most successful compound locomotives ever to run in Britain.

Johnson gave up his post at the end of 1903 and Deeley took over until August 1909 when he resigned, but in the space of those few years he introduced the '990' class 4-4-0s with his own design of valve gear (ostensibly to prove that a 'simple' engine could equal a 'compound' in performance), two steam motor coaches for the MR's Morecame-Heysham line and built jointly by the Locomotive and Carriage & Wagon Works and some 0-6-0 tender engines.

In 1907 a new class of 40 0-6-4T engines, originally designed for goods work and then changed to become a powerful suburban type, appeared from the Works and soon became nicknamed 'Flatirons' on account of their square shape and heavy and ponderous appearance, although Nottingham and Lincoln men referred to them as 'Pom-Poms'.

In January 1909 Derby Works turned out the revolutionary Paget 2-6-2 experimental locomotive No 2299, brainchild of and paid for by Cecil Walter Paget, son of the MR Chairman and appointed MR 'General Superintendent' on 5 April 1907. He and Deeley had frequent disagreements as when Paget wished overtime to be worked on his engine at MR expense. Upon Deeley refusing to sanction this, Cecil Paget replied 'Well, we'll see what Father says then'.

Deeley resigned when informed that his post of Locomotive Superintendent was to be split into two (Chief Mechanical Engineer and Chief Motive Power Superintendent) and Henry Fowler took over the former of the new posts.

During Fowler's term of office the first of an enlarged 0-6-0 type goods tender engine, No 3835, with a Class G7 superheated boiler appeared in October 1911. The famous 0-10-0 Lickey banking engine No 2290, appeared in December 1919 and a batch of six 2-8-0 heavy freight tender engines designed for working mineral traffic on the Somerset & Dorset Joint line, was built between February and July 1914. In addition, a major rebuilding exercise

was put in hand for the earlier 4-4-0s, fitting them with new frames and Class G7 boilers with Schmidt superheaters.

On the Carriage & Wagon front a new heavier pattern of carriage was built at Derby in 1897 which was to become a hallmark of MR carriage construction. 8ft 6in wide in the body, it had 1st class compartments 7ft 9in long as against the 3rd class at 6ft 6in. In 1899 the first trains of 50ft corridor carriages were turned out for joint stock expresses and by the end of the century the Works had an output of eight new passenger carriages and 180 new wagons per week.

Above:
Fowler's famous 0-10-0 Lickey Banker No 2290 completed at Derby in December 1919 and nick-named 'Big Bertha'.
MR Official, Author's Collection

Below:
Paget's 2-6-2 experimental locomotive No 2299 completed at Derby in January 1909. It had two cylinder blocks between the driving axles with opposed pistons driven by rotary valve gear.
MR Official, Author's Collection

Clayton retired in December 1901 to be replaced by David Bain from the North Eastern Railway. Further expansion of the Works took place in 1908 and in 1910 electric power was introduced to drive both machinery and overhead cranes, power being supplied from the new power station in the Derby Locomotive Works which itself was 'electrified' at the same time.

Bain designed new sleeping and dining cars, some with clipper bodies, but all superbly finished both inside and out and in 1908 was also responsible for the design of carriage stock for the newly electrified Morecambe, Heysham and Lancaster line.

In 1912 the Works turned out the first and only Royal Saloon for the MRs Royal Train, No 1910, which fortunately survives today in the care of the Midland Railway Trust at Butterley.

With the outbreak of World War 1 both Works became involved in the war effort, the carriage works providing eight ambulance

Above left:
A crowded paint shop at Derby Locomotive Works as it appeared on 13 March 1914.
MR Official, Author's Collection

Above:
A large steam hammer busily at work in the Carriage & Wagon works forge about 1896.
MR Official, Author's Collection

Below:
Interior of the then new lifting shop, now called 'U' shop, at Derby Carriage & Wagon works as it was on 19 July 1910.
MR Official, Author's Collection

trains, a large number of 20 ton covered wagons, vehicles for carrying tanks and armoured vehicles and modified some 6,000 vehicles for overseas use in addition to a large quantity of road vehicle conversions including 1,500 general service wagons, water carts, stretchers and 250,000 stampings for rifle parts. Bain went to London in June 1915 to take charge of a Ministry Department and

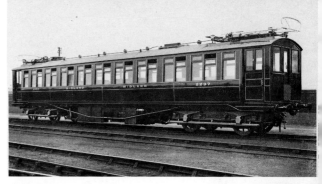

Above right:
Electric motor car No 2237 built for the Lancaster-Heysham services at Derby in 1907.
MR Official courtesy Midland Railway Trust Ltd

Right:
All for the war-effort . . . a group of stout-hearted females rest momentarily from their labours stacking coal on No 4 shed at Derby on 3 May 1917. *MR Official, Author's Collection*

Below:
Women at work in the special shop set aside in the locomotive works for the renovation of 18 pounder brass cartridge cases, c1916.
MR Official, Author's Collection

Robert Whyte Reid took over in April 1916 eventually permanently succeeding Bain after his brief return at the war's end.

The Locomotive Works manufactured howitzer cradles, limbers and carriages and flanged plates for guns and fuse parts, a special shop being devoted to the renovation of 18 pounder brass cartridge cases, weekly output being no less than 130,000.

After the war the Locomotive Works continued building 0-6-0 tender engines and the Carriage Works Reid developments of Bain's stock, this time with semi-eliptical roofs, some superb first and third class dining carriages for the MR and M&GSW stock, several lots of 48ft bogie carriages for London suburban service and some 57ft corridor vehicles as well as continuing the output of a large variety of goods, mineral and cattle wagons and special purpose vehicles.

On 1 January, 1923 the MR disappeared to become part of the new London Midland & Scottish Railway Co. The Locomotive Works turned out more of the Class 4 0-6-0 goods

Above:
The first of Fowler's 2-6-2T engines seen here in March 1930 when almost new.
LMS Official, Author's Collection

Below:
The first of the Derby built 'Royal Scot' class 4-6-0s No 6150 *The Life Guardsman* which was completed in June 1930.
LMS Official, Author's Collection

engines, and began building more compounds in February, 1924 but apart from some 4-4-2T engines for the London, Tilbury & Southend section of line, the first of which was only in the erecting shop for 11 days, there was no share in the building of new LMS designs until the first of Fowler's 2-6-4 passenger tank engines No 2300, emerged in December 1927 followed by No 563, the first of the LMS version of the 4-4-0 standard light passenger express locomotive based on earlier MR designs, which was completed in March 1928, and 10 0-6-0 dock tank engines Nos 11270-9, in

December 1928. The year 1930 saw the emergence of No 15500, the first of the new suburban 2-6-2T engines, and in June Derby showed its capabilities by producing the first of a batch of 20 'Royal Scot' class 4-6-0 locomotives numbered 6150-6169, the engine being completed in a record time of 26 days from the laying down of the frames to it leaving the works ready for traffic, an achievement which proved the value of the progressive system of scheduling work in all shops to specific timescales.

Days on Works were cut down by five to 20 by using exchange boilers repaired in advance for an engine being shopped, and the number of engines on Works at any one time was reduced from between 260 and 300 to between 60 and 65. Output was 20 general repairs per week, four engines in and out per day, the balance being dealt with on Saturday mornings.

Hard on the heels of the Scots came the first of the 'Patriot' class 4-6-0s, 'rebuilt' (in theory at least) from the 'Claughton' class of the LNWR, the first of which, No 5971, left the Works in November 1930. Twelve of these were built in all, two in 1930 and the remainder in 1933 between February and May, after William Stanier had arrived on the scene to take the LMS Locomotive policy in hand and urgently produce some new and more powerful designs of passenger and mixed traffic engines. Derby was to have no share in this, and only produced 10 0-4-4T engines described by E. S. Cox as the final fling of MR mystique.

Above:
The wheel-dressing section of No 8 erecting shop at Derby Locomotive Works on 28 July 1928. Here the various wheelsets were fitted up prior to the re-wheeling of a repaired locomotive.
LMS Official, Author's Collection

Below:
LMS 'Baby Scot' 4-6-0 No 5963, later renumbered 5526 and eventually named *Morecambe and Heysham* in 1937, seen here brand new out of the Derby shops in March 1933.
The late Frank Carrier, Author's Collection

Forerunner of the modern diesel-shunter, this prototype, No 1831 was rebuilt from a Johnson 0-6-0T steam locomotive at Derby in 1932.
LMS Official, Author's Collection

Below:
Where it all began — the CME's Locomotive Drawing Office where all new scheming and design work was done and where new production drawings and subsequent modifications were prepared.
LMS Official, Author's Collection

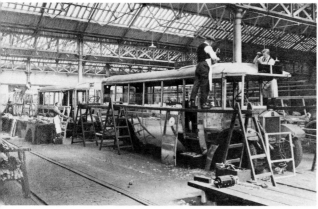

Stanier concentrated all new boiler construction at Crewe leaving Derby with boiler repair work only.

A batch of 10 'Jubilee' class 4-6-0s in December 1934 was followed by 54 Class 5 4-6-0s in 1943-4, but the bulk of this period's output was 2-6-2T and 2-6-4T engines, Class 2 4-4-0 passenger tender engines and 0-6-0 goods tender engines.

However, Derby was to be the focal point for the first LMS trials of diesel power. One of Johnsons 0-6-0T engines, No 1831, was rebuilt as an 0-6-0 diesel-hydraulic locomotive with a Davey-Paxman 400bhp six-cylinder diesel engine and Haslam & Newton hydrostatic transmission.

Trials with this locomotive, which due to transmission problems had a life of only seven years, and later trials with 11 other diesel shunting locomotives produced by outside firms, resulted in the introduction of the LMS 0-6-0 diesel shunting locomotive, this time with English Electric engines and electric transmission with jackshaft drive to the driving wheels. The first No 7080, emerged from Derby in May 1939 and, with a change to direct gear drive in 1944, the Works continued to produce them as a basic type for both the LMS and the War Department, and with a somewhat modified design, they continued to be produced for British Railways at Derby as the standard design until 1960.

Some time before this in 1928, the old

Left:
Not only carriages and wagons but also road vehicles of various types were built at the Derby Carriage and Wagon Works as this production line for LMS Albion buses in 'C' shop in 1929 shows. *LMS Official, Author's Collection*

Above:
The bodysides of Stanier wooden-framed corridor brake coach are here being cramped to the solebar in this view taken in March 1935.
LMS Official, Author's Collection

Right:
The wagon building shop at Derby Carriage & Wagon works in 1936 showing the layout for mass production. *LMS Official, Author's Collection*

locomotive drawing office in the Works had been moved from the main offices into a separate building known as 'The Stables' but in August 1931 they joined forces with their Carriage & Wagon colleagues occupying the ground and first floors respectively of a building on the London Road adjacent to the original Carriage & Wagon Works offices whose staff were now re-located in an office block within the Works itself.

The Carriage & Wagon Works had switched from wooden-bodied carriages to all steel coaches and in 1927 a new design of 1st class corridor coach with no outside compartment doors was built, whilst further sleeping cars of the 3rd class and composite types continued to be produced.

However, in the late 1920s part of the Works was given over to road motor vehicles, fitting bodies to Karrier and Morris vans and lorries whilst in 1928 a batch of single-deck buses emerged on Leyland Lion chassis followed in 1929 by others on 'Albion' chassis.

In 1930 the first LMS dining cars produced at Derby appeared, and Derby produced large quantities of new LMS designs between 1924 and 1951 including 1,064 3rd class corridor brakes, 594 3rd class corridor coaches, 355 composite corridor coaches, 33 1st class

corridor brakes and 13 1st class corridor coaches and also built 1,211 3rd class, 91 3rd brakes, 50 composites and 116 1st class 'open' type stock between 1923 and 1939.

Mass production of wagons was by now giving a weekly (5½ day) output of 200 open wagons, 20 cattle wagons and 47 covered goods wagons, and in addition the Works was turning out seven new carriages per week. Total output of wagons between 1923 and the introduction of the 16-ton all steel mineral wagon in 1945 amounted to more than 62,000 12-ton mineral and open wagons, 9,500 covered vans, 3,400 goods brake vans and 2,300 cattle wagons.

At this time the Works was using over a million cubic feet of timber annually compared to 2½ million in MR days! In 1930 all drop stamping work for the LMS was concentrated

at the Works with an output of 35-40 tons per week whilst the iron foundry was producing 200 tons of castings per week and the nut and bolt shop 26 tons of bolts and 3¼ tons of nuts each 5½ days!

By 1932 the Works occupied 128 acres of which 36 were under cover and had a staff of some 3,400 of which 140 were female,

employed as clerks and in trimming seats and polishing panelling, etc.

Stanier's arrival initiated the first all-welded steel underframes and bogies in 1934 and decorative beading disappeared in favour of flat sheet steel. In 1937 11 three-car articulated sets of vehicles were constructed at Derby and a further 55 two-coach sets were built for trial on the Central Division of the LMS, whilst in March the following year a streamlined three-car articulated railcar was built at Derby.

It was powered by six 125bhp Leyland engines with Lysholm Smith hydraulic transmission and utilised low-alloy high tensile steels for both underframes and bogies. Its trials were unfortunately interrupted by the war, it never took centre stage and 26 years

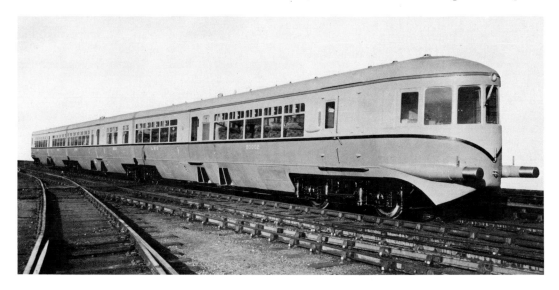

were to elapse before the diesel railcar made its re-appearance in the Works. Trial runs took place between Euston and Tring and it was later based at Bedford working regular services between St Pancras and Nottingham.

During the first few years of World War 2, some 152 passenger stock vehicles were built for the Liverpool-Southport electrified line and work continued on a variety of goods, mineral and special types.

Both Works were again involved in the war effort, the Carriage Works sharing with Wolverton the production of 66 special trains for home and overseas use by the Allied Forces, and at Derby sections of aircraft were both built and repaired, 2,878 pairs of aeroplane wings being produced in 'B' Shop and 1,000 pairs of 'Typhoon' aircraft wings in 'E' shop as well as others for 'Tempest' and 'Roc' aeroplanes. 'A' shop was also set up for

the repair of fuselages for 'Whitley', 'Hampden' and 'Lancaster' bombers and 'Spitfire' fighters.

The Locomotive Works was involved, amongst other things, in the production of 25 and 17 pounder Field guns for the army, searchlight projectors, tank seats and turrets, Bailey bridge panels, bomb casings and the renovation of shell cases, and women were taken on in Derby Shops for the second time to cope with the workload.

In 1943-4 54 of Stanier's famous 'Black Five' 4-6-0 locomotives Nos 5472-99 and 4800-25 were built at Derby — one of the locomotive types which 'won the war on the Railways'.

After the war the Locomotive Works produced a new variety of 2-6-4T locomotives designed by C. E. Fairburn, who had stood in for Stanier's absence on war service but who died in October 1945.

H. G. Ivatt took his place on 1 February 1946 and set up his office at Derby. His first design was for a 5ft 3in gauge 2-6-4T for the Northern Counties Committee (of Ireland) of the LMS for which Derby built 18 between 1946 and 1950.

However, the most far reaching event at Derby was the appearance on 5 December 1947 of No 10000, proudly carrying the letters 'LMS' on its sides, the first main line diesel-electric locomotive to be built in Britain, closely followed by its twin, No 10001, the following July. Ivatt, on behalf of the LMS, had combined resources with the English Electric Co in order to produce these two 1,600hp prototypes capable of working as a coupled unit and after trials the pair made an inaugural non-stop run on the 'Royal Scot' between London Euston and Glasgow on 1 June 1949. Construction of the locomotives was carried out in No 10A diesel shop, once part of the paint shop and now specially set aside for the construction of diesel locomotives.

The Carriage Works had recommenced work in 1944 on the remaining 'Coronation Scot' carriages begun before the war, and they eventually entered service in 1947, although not on Anglo-Scottish expresses as originally intended.

On 1 January 1948 the railway centre of Derby found itself part of the national system as 'British Railways' came into being. Old pre-grouping loyalties to the MR still survived even after 25 years of the LMS (and survive today!) and these were to be tried even further as Derby now vied for work with the railway manufacturing centres of the LNER, GWR and SR.

The outcome of this fascinating 'struggle' will be the subject of a later chapter.

Above:
Wheeling 5ft 3in gauge 2-6-4T locomotive No 50 being built for the Northern Counties Committee of the LMS in No 3 bay of No 8 erecting shop at Derby in April 1949.
BR Official, Author's Collection

Below:
LMS diesel-shunting locomotives under repair in the No 10A diesel shop at Derby Locomotive Works. *Derby Museums*

Below:
Britain's first main line diesel-electric locomotive No 10000, completed at Derby by the LMS in December 1947, its twin No 10001, emerging the following July.
LMS Official, Author's Collection

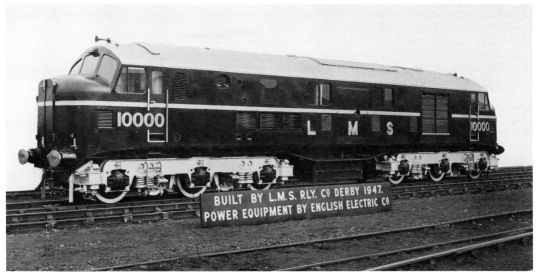

The development of lines and traffic (1850-1922)

Such was the geographically pivotal position of Derby as a railway centre that it was initially through the acquisition of other companies' lines or running powers by the MR and the building of extensions to existing lines rather than developments in the Derby area, that governed the considerable and rapid growth of traffic passing through in the first decades of the new company's history.

On 8 February 1845, George Hudson, Chairman of the MR, prompted by John Ellis, his far-seeing deputy, signed an agreement with the Birmingham & Gloucester and Bristol & Gloucester Railway companies (who were themselves in the process of amalgamating into one company, even though the Bristol Co had broad gauge tracks and both had almost been acquired by the Great Western Co). This consolidated both companies in the MR in return for a guaranteed 6% upon their capital and thereby secured for the MR an entry to Bristol. Thus was added another leg of a great through route which was to stretch from Bristol through Derby to the North of England. The Act vesting the two companies in the MR was passed on 3 August 1846, and not only added the 54 miles or so of Birmingham & Gloucester 'narrow' gauge (ie 4ft 8½in) tracks, its stations, locomotives and rolling stock, together with the right of running powers into the LNWR station at Curzon Street, Birmingham, but also the 30 miles of broad gauge (7ft ½in) track of the Bristol and Gloucester company which ran from a junction with the GWR at Bristol, with powers to run into their Temple Meads station, to Standish Junction near Stonehouse, with further powers to run over the Cheltenham & Great Western Union Railway into Gloucester station.

As to Birmingham — when the LNWR opened New Street station on 1 June 1854, the MR took up a right under the Birmingham & Gloucester Companies Act to run into Curzon Street station 'or any future termination at or near Birmingham' and by making an extensive curve a mile in length, constructed under an Act of 27 July 1846, connected Saltley on the old B&DJR line with the LNWR at 'Derby Junction' adjacent to New Street station. In 1848 the Midland had obtained powers to make a new 'narrow gauge' line from Gloucester to Standish Junction and to lay a third rail to give mixed gauge to Bristol Temple Meads and this was opened on 29 May 1854, giving a narrow gauge through route from Leeds to Bristol. Thus was forged the great and still unique 'West road', now called the northeast-southwest route, of considerble advantage even to present day travellers, with Derby an important junction with other intersecting railway routes at the mid-point.

Below:
Early MR excursion leaflet for a trip from Derby to London, Euston with a very early starting time of 5.15am. *Author's Collection*

By 1851 services to and from Derby had become quite complex. On weekdays to Leeds the 6am stopping passenger took 3hr 40min for the 74-mile journey calling at 20 stations en route, whilst the mail train covered the distance in just three hours, and the fastest express, at 12.45pm, took only 2hr with stops at Eckington, Masboro' and Normanton.

The best train from Leeds, the 10.15am, took a mere 2hr 10min to reach Derby. The total of services from Derby to the North comprised two mails at 2.15am and 3.50pm and six passenger trains to Leeds; two passengers to Ambergate; 10 goods trains, two running along to Normanton and one to Eckington; one mineral to Masboro'; one coal train to Staveley and one to Clay Cross; one empty coke train to Normanton and an empty wagon train to Staveley.

Sunday services to Leeds consisted of two mail trains at 2.15am and 3.45pm and two

passengers at 6.45am and 5pm with a local to Ambergate at 9am, and three goods trains, two to Normanton at 9pm and 10.30pm and one to Eckington at 11.30pm.

At Ambergate passengers could join the trains of the Manchester, Buxton, Matlock & Midlands Junction Railway which had opened its first stretch of line between Ambergate and Rowsley on 4 June 1849. This route was later to be extended by the MR to Buxton and Manchester. Six trains ran each way daily in connection with services from Derby or Leeds, with one on Sunday each way.

Services between Derby and Nottingham consisted of eight trains of which four ran on to Lincoln in a best time of 2hr 15min with a mail train at 2.20am calling at Nottingham (2.55am) and Newark (4am) and which covered the 48¾ miles in 2hr and 35min.

Three goods trains ran each way between Derby and Lincoln with one between Nottingham and Derby only at 8pm. On Sunday in addition to the mail trains two passenger trains ran in each direction leaving Derby at 7.30am and 5.40pm.

The linking passenger service to London Euston via Rugby had departures from Derby at 6am (mail), 8.30am, 11am, 12.35pm, 2.05pm, 3.20pm, 4.15pm, an express at 6.25pm which reached Rugby in 1hr 25min with a stop at Leicester only, and another mail at 11.07pm. There were, in addition, two coal and seven goods and mineral trains of which two were express. Similar services ran in the reverse direction.

In the Birmingham direction passenger trains ran at 8am, 11.05am, 2.15pm, 4pm and 6.30pm covering the 41¼ miles in a best time of 1hr 50min with stops at Burton, Tamworth and Whitacre. Four goods and two mineral trains ran and there was a mail train at 11.17pm reaching Birmingham in 2hr 33min. Two passenger trains and one mail train ran each way on Sundays with an extra goods to Derby at 3am. Three early morning goods trains ran from Birmingham at 2am, 3am and 3.45am with five passenger trains, a mail train at 11.20pm, a further goods at 10.15pm, an empty wagons train at 7.15pm and a morning goods and empty wagon train at 9.30am. Passengers travelling beyond Birmingham made separate connections there for the MR's newly acquired extension to Gloucester and Bristol.

Midland traffic of all kinds was expanding rapidly and on 2 December, 1851 its Board heard a report from John Fox Bell, Joseph Sanders, W. H. Barlow and Matthew Kirtley regarding delays to trains at Derby. There

Below:
A later excursion, this time to the GNR's station at King's Cross via Hitchin and with an even earlier 5.00am starting time! *Author's Collection*

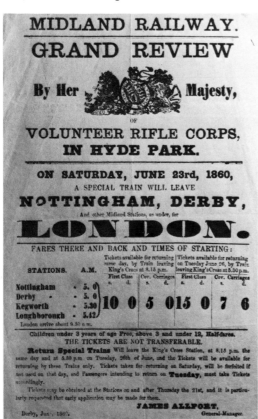

Above:
The MR's town goods shed at St Mary's goods yard. *Author*

being no rail arrangements outside the station for sorting traffic, trains that could otherwise remain outside had to enter the station for shunting, and other trains were 'therefore compelled to stand upon the Bank'. At each shunt the engine had to traverse backwards and forwards by means of the arrival passenger line, a process interrupted by the arrival of each passenger train and therefore many goods and mineral trains, which should have been ready to pass forward in a few minutes, were delayed up to 1½hr before being able to proceed. The group also reported on the great difficulty in accommodating local goods and mineral traffic in Derby Yard.

As a remedy, sorting sidings outside Derby Yard were recommended along with an extension of the then goods wharf on to MR land between Siddals Lane and the Derby Canal to facilitate loading and unloading of traffic. At that time some 23,000 tons of mineral traffic was being handled annually at Derby Wharf, the whole of which had to pass through the station to the coal wharf, even if only one wagon required to be detached. The group saw no remedy but that a wharf be made near St Mary's Bridge in conjunction with the new Ripley extension of the Little Eaton branch.

It was hoped thereby that the mill and

foundry owners mainly located near to the bridge, then being put off collecting coal from the wharf beyond the station because of distance, would switch from canal to rail not only for receiving their supplies of coal and coke but for dispatching their heavy goods and castings. The Engineer costed the St Mary's sidings at £10,000 and the extension sidings to Siddals Lane at £3,000.

Sir Joseph Paxton responded on 2 February 1852, with a recommendation that three new sidings only be constructed at the North Junction, the South Junction and the London Road Bridge, each 400yd long and at a cost of £1,200, and this cheaper option was adopted. It was to be another 3½ years before the separate St Mary's branch and goods station was provided along with its sidings as a relief to the situation.

On 6 June 1854, Mr Barlow was asked to submit a plan and estimate for the sidings required to sort mineral trains from the Erewash, Leicester and Burton lines following Mr Markham's report. This was done on 4 July 1854 but was postponed for further discussion.

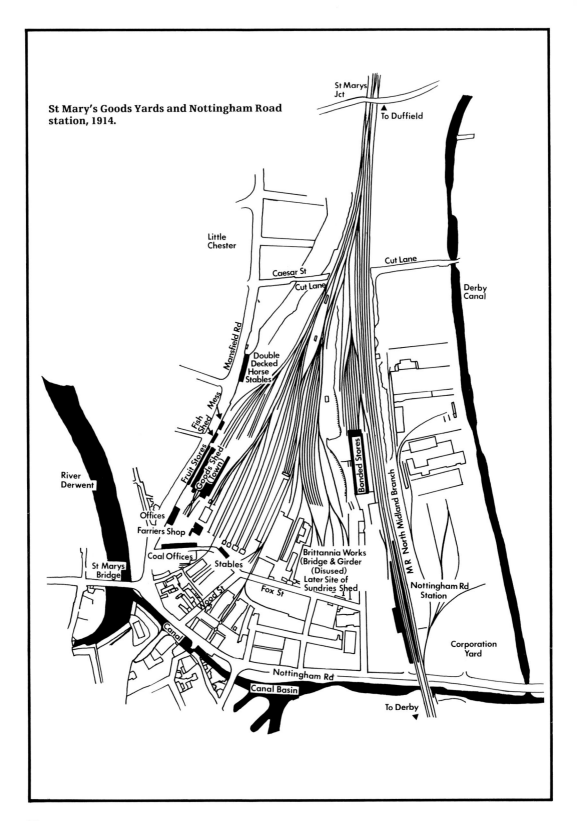

St Mary's Goods Yards and Nottingham Road station, 1914.

Little Chester

Caesar St

Cut Lane

Cut Lane

Derby Canal

Mansfield Rd

Double Decked Horse Stables

Fish Shed

Mess.

Fruit Stores

Goods Shed (Town)

River Derwent

Offices

Farriers Shop

Coal Offices

St Marys Bridge

Stables

Wood St

Fox St

Brittannia Works (Bridge & Girder) (Disused) Later Site of Sundries Shed

Bonded Stores

M.R. North Midland Branch

Nottingham Rd Station

Corporation Yard

Canal

Nottingham Rd

Canal Basin

To Derby

St Marys Jct

To Duffield

Above:

The last remnants of the once extensive coal merchants' stock piles at St Mary's goods yard in September 1985. *Author*

The half mile St Mary's Goods station branch, which was double tracked, was eventually built under the same Act of 1848 which sanctioned the construction of the Ripley branch, and ran from St Mary's Junction, 54 chains north of Derby station, to a large goods station adjacent to St Mary's bridge over the Derwent where an extensive wharf was established to distribute coal brought from the collieries on the Ripley branch for use in the town. The goods branch opened for traffic in September 1855 just before the Ripley extension with which its construction was linked, and its facilities were gradually developed over the years. A new coal office, goods shed, grain shed and more sidings were added in 1861-2.

Under the Midland's Additional Powers Act of 1862 St Mary's was further enlarged on newly acquired land. New offices, a corn store and a goods warehouse were all built by Thompson and Fryer in 1862 with machinery and hoistings supplied by Armstrong & Co, and new stables were built by Edward Dusautoy, a local builder of Summerhill, Victoria Street.

Further land was acquired in 1863, the land fenced and levelled and more new sidings added at a cost of £2,035/5s/0d with earth moving and ballasting undertaken from May 1862 and the laying of permanent way at a cost of a further £11,059 from November 1862. Work continued on the sidings complex until early in 1868.

Other additions included further sidings in 1866, a potato store in 1867 at a cost of some £1,450, further goods sidings in 1869 at a cost

of £1,780 and a major expansion of the sidings and goods wharf area on land acquired from Edward Dusautoy at a total cost of some £8,000 in 1876.

With the coming of the railway and the development of goods yards, Derby's dependence on local produce was reduced and meat, fish and perishable foods could quickly be brought into the town as well as cereal crops, resulting in the eventual closure of the Corn Exchange in Albert Street (opened 20 January 1862) around 1880.

Concurrent with the developments at St Mary's further land alongside the former MCR line through Chaddesden had been acquired and by 1860 work was in hand levelling, forming culverts and other earthworks. Permanent way at a cost of £13,751, plus a further £1,668 for ballasting, was being installed later that year in a programme which continued until June 1862, and other developments followed to the end of 1863. Signals and pointsmen's boxes had already been installed by mid-1860 and new buildings including offices, and stables for horses were built between October 1861 and December 1863 at a cost of £2,043/18s/11d. A second set of sorting sidings, No 2 was installed as a follow-on scheme, work commencing at the end of 1861.

Further major developments at Chaddesden Sidings began in 1871 with a consideration of quadrupling the main line, but this was

Above:
The double-decked horse stables at St Mary's goods yard, erected in 1862 and now in use for other purposes, in part as a pallet manufactory.
Author

Further work at St Mary's goods depot included a shipping and delivery office, approved on 5 November 1872, at a cost of £500, and an extensive stable block for dray horses at a cost of £1,150 which was agreed on 1 July 1873.

Meanwhile, improvements in the MR's services to London from Derby had come about in two main stages. By means of the Act of 4 August 1853, it was authorised to construct a line from Leicester via Bedford to a junction with the GNR's main line near Hitchin in Hertfordshire, thereby giving access to that company's King's Cross station, the line opening for mineral traffic on 15 April 1857, with goods traffic a week later and passenger services to King's Cross commencing on Thursday, 7 May, although the MR continued to use Euston station for a number of years for services running via Rugby over the old MCR route.

Through running powers into King's Cross only came on 1 February, 1858 but the MR and GNR were decidedly unhappy bed-fellows, the GNR frustrating the prompt arrival of MR trains on many occasions, holding up even passenger traffic at Hitchin in favour of its own goods services. Finally the MR decided the situation was intolerable and began construction of an independent route across virgin country from Bedford to serve a new and magnificent London terminus at St Pancras. The Act to construct the station was passed on 25 May 1860, the new railway was authorised by an Act of 22 June 1863, and was

postponed on 28 February. Additional sidings, No 3, were finally approved by the Board at a cost of £15,263 on 4 February, 1873 and sidings were also agreed to on 2 December, 1873 at a cost of £3,730 to serve the new Wagon Repair Shops, approval of which, at a cost of £6,868, had been given the previous year on 2 October. On 11 October, 1873, stabling for 20 horses was agreed for erection at a cost of £950, and a suite of goods offices at a cost of £250 was agreed to on 3 June 1873.

A further major item appeared on 1 July 1873 — a 12-road wooden shed 680ft×150ft wide, to house sleeping carriages erected, at the Spondon end of the Chaddesden complex at a cost of £1,320. It was still largely intact in the 1950s.

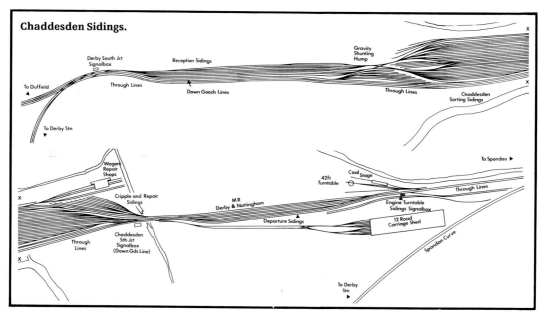

Chaddesden Sidings.

formally opened on 7 September 1867, regular traffic commencing Monday 9 September.

Services between Derby and London in 1860 involved both King's Cross and Euston and trains left at 6am (arriving King's Cross at 10.05am and Euston at 10.30); 8.10am (1.35 and 1.50); 10.15am (ex-Leeds at 6am Government class and 7.40am 1st and 2nd class)(3.50 and 3.30); 11.50am (3.50 and 4.5); 2.25pm (8.00 and 6.25); 4.15pm (Euston 9.15) 6.40pm (10.20 and 10.50); and 12.35am (Euston only at 5.5am).

Other developments in the Derby area were confined to the building of branch lines to link with some of the outlying populated areas in the locality. North of Derby the 6 miles 47 chains Ripley branch opened to passenger traffic on 1 September, 1856 with intermediate stations at Little Eaton, Coxbench, Kilburn and 'Denbey' (sic) and Ripley (old station) 'where an omnibus from the Thorn Tree Inn meets all of the trains for outlying parts'. Goods traffic had commenced using the branch the previous year.

This branch was an extension of the original

Above:
Stanier Class 8F 2-8-0 No 48062 heads out of Chaddesden Sidings on 24 June 1955 with a train of 22 wagons. *BR Official*

Below:
Kirtley 2-2-2 No 28, one of the '30' class Singles built at Derby in 1864 for use on Leicester to King's Cross services.
MR Official, Author's Collection

Above:
Coxbench station on the Little Eaton and Ripley branch. *Author*

Below:
Derby Nottingham Road station, decorated specially for the Royal Show of June 1906 which was held in the town that year.
MR Official, Crown Copyright
courtesy National Railway Museum

Little Eaton branch railway, only 25 chains long, which had its termination near the stone quarries and the arm of the Derby Canal in that village, and which had been opened in the early part of 1848 at a cost of some £4,200.

On 1 May 1855 Mr Allport recommended that 'there should be a passenger station on the Nottingham Road' in connection with the Ripley branch and this was agreed by the Chairmen's Committee.

The new station opened on 1 September, 1856 and proved so popular that platforms were soon extended and a waiting shed built by John Wood of Derby in August 1860 at a cost of £130/6s/2d. Further extensions were made early in 1867 and in September, 1868

another bill was met for still further enlarging the platforms. On 31 August 1869, Smith Brothers received £3/5s/5d for 'a new iron urinal' for installation at the station.

Periodically the station was extra busy in connection with Derby Races for the new racecourse situated only a short distance away had been opened in August 1848, the MR subsequently providing a special siding and horse dock landing to serve the Course. In 1885 William White was its stationmaster.

A few miles to the north a new branch line was created from Duffield, and the station there moved a little to the south, in order to make a rail link with Wirksworth in the stone uplands of Derbyshire, and also provide a possible alternative route beyond there to Rowsley. This was done in case the jointly leased MBM&MJR from there southwards to Ambergate fell into the hands of the LNWR rather than the Midland who were already constructing a line north of Rowsley to link with Buxton and New Mills by Acts of 1860 and 1862 respectively.

The eight miles 29 chains Wirksworth branch, which broadly follows the River Ecclesbourne, was eventually opened on 1 October 1867 with intermediate stations at Hazlewood, Shottle and Idridgehay with a service of two statutory 'Government' trains and one 1st and 2nd class only train daily each way and no Sunday service.

To the south of Derby came further lines including those to Melbourne and Ashby, constructed as two separate railways but opened in three stages and built to connect Derby with the market gardening centre around Melbourne and the limestone, coal and clayware centres of northwest Leicestershire.

In May 1864, the 'New Lines and Additional Powers Bill' received Parliamentary approval

and authorised the building of a section from Melbourne Junction, just west of Pear Tree and Normanton station and on the line to Birmingham, to an end-on connection with the existing Ashby and Cloud Hill ('Ticknall') Tramway at Breedon, a distance of 9 miles 9½ chains. A short branch of 48½ chains at Normanton, planned to form a south to west curve, was never actually built, the site being subsequently occupied by a brickworks.

Due to heavy financial commitments, further railway construction was delayed and the section from Melbourne Junction to Melbourne did not open for traffic until 1 September 1868, followed by Melbourne to Worthington on 1 October 1869 and finally, Worthington to Ashby on 1 January 1874.

The Ashby & Cloud Hill Tramway, originally built by Benjamin Outram at a cost of £31,600 opened in part in 1799 and was completed by 1 May, 1805. The Act for making the Ashby-de-la-Zouch canal was passed on 9 May 1794 and Clause 18 gave the original company power to build means other than canals 'to such place or places in the said line as they shall think proper'.

Thus radiating from the Willesley basin end of the canal (which joined the Coventry Canal at Marston Bridge in Warwickshire), a number of tramroads came to be built, one of which was to Ticknall lime works a distance of 8¾ miles with a branch some 4¼ miles long to Cloud Hill.

The MR purchased the property of the Ashby Canal Co for £110,000 by an Act of 16 July 1846 and a further Act of 5 July 1865 authorised the conversion of the Ashby and Cloud Hill section from a 4ft 2in gauge flanged-rail tramway to a standard (4ft 8½in) gauge railway. However, the branch to Ticknall lime works was not converted and remained in use, if only latterly

Above:
Mishap at Melbourne Junction as Kirtley straight-framed 0-6-0 No 261 lands in the cess with its train in a jumble.
MR Official, Author's Collection

Below:
The Derby cattle market was served by the MR's cattle docks situated just to the north of Derby station and is seen here on 26 November 1909.
MR Official, Author's Collection

by 'right-of-way' journeys, until 20 May 1913.

The converted section, which was built in part on a new alignment due to the unsuitability of the tramway's civil engineering, served a modest branch platform some distance from the main Ashby station and the 447yd long Old Parks tunnel, beyond Ashby, was rebored to take main line traffic.

Inter-linking with the new line, and on common metals between Chellaston East and West Junctions came the line from Sheet Stores Junction, near to Trent Junction, and joining the Derby to Birmingham main line at Stenson Junction providing an important cross-country route. The section from Sheet

Stores Junction to Weston-on-Trent was authorised by the Additional Powers Act of 5 July 1865 but even before it had been completed the other leg to Stenson Junction had also been authorised. The final section was opened to Stenson Junction on 3 November 1873 following opening of the section from Sheet Stores Junction to Chellaston East Junction on 6 December, 1869, making a link with the Derby-Melbourne line.

The NSR commendably seized the opportunity to extend their limited passenger network by initiating a through service between Liverpool and Nottingham (by virtue of running powers) using this new route from 1874, six new composite coaches being built for the purpose.

In the Derby station area a fourth line had been added early in 1857 between what was later Derby North Junction and Five Arches bridge over the river in order to ease traffic movements and three cross-over roads were installed on the curves at Derby, to avoid the necessity of traffic entering the Derby Yard, at a cost of £1,000. However, there were still only the two original tracks crossing the Five Arches bridge, causing considerable constriction of traffic flow.

On 3 January 1860, the MR Board agreed to construct a cattle station on its own land midway between the main Derby and the Nottingham Road stations, having the necessary communications with the railway and also, at the company's expense, to construct and maintain two roads and provide half of the cost of a bridge over the Derwent (up to a maximum of £500) to connect with the new Derby Cattle Market. However, on 1 August 1860 the Board agreed to construct the bridge at a width of 30ft at their own expense and make and maintain two 36ft roadways in return for Derby Corporation relieving the MR of any obligation to repair the old Meadow Lane.

One particular difficulty at Derby station related to the horse dock which was situated on ground opposite the present Institute, where the rails were lowered to facilitate the loading of private carriages and horses. Since there was then only a single passenger platform, turntables were situated on the through lines to get the carriage trucks and horse boxes into the dock, and a movable wooden section of the main platform on wheels had to be moved out of the way each time a horse box or other vehicle had to be dealt with.

In an attempt to increase platform accommodation the Birmingham end of the Derby platform was extended in June 1862 and in the same year the goods lines in the Derby Yard were further altered to improve traffic flow, a new 'signal and point box' being installed at the north end of the station.

To the south of Derby station a new and important length of line, Spondon Curve, one mile 77 chains long, was constructed and opened on 27 June 1867, linking that end of the station at London Road Junction with the old MCR line just north of Spondon station at Spondon Junction, with a swing bridge built near Deadman's Lane to carry the line over the Derby Canal.

Its opening facilitated the running of passenger trains from the south to the north directly through Derby station and vice-versa for the first time, since before that date trains had had to run into Derby via the old MCR line and Chaddesden arriving in the station facing towards Birmingham and the west. Therefore a fresh engine had to be provided at what had been the rear to take the trains forward, these having at first to run along a line outside the station before being reversed into the sole platform from the west.

The movement of traffic originating from the south and not requiring to pass through Derby station was also greatly eased by the construction of yet another short link line, only 23 chains long, between Derby South Junction and Derby North Junction. This was opened on 1 November 1866, and enabled trains to avoid Derby altogether and pass via Chaddesden on the old MCR route and thence via the new link directly on to the old NMR line just south of Derby Nottingham Road station.

The opening of this link was not without its own particular tragedy for George Henry Rickman, the Derby stationmaster, stood in the path of the first train in a moment's forgetfulness and was run over and killed. The driver of the train, a Nottingham man named William Elliott, had the misfortune of being concerned in a greater number of fatal accidents than any other driver, through no fault of his own.

The working of the then single platformed station at Derby was a complex matter for there was no inter-locking of points and few signals save one having an enormous arm and located at the end of the station building which fell with a loud clang! The pointsman or 'bobby' on duty at the north end had an alcove near to the Cheese Warehouse from which he would emerge in his shining top hat to signal trains in and out of the station.

Shunters and goods guards had to scurry about changing sets of points in sequence to

facilitate a train movement and also to operate the many small turntables located at the intersection of the various through lines and the lateral servicing lines, thereby enabling stock to be moved from any part of one line to another. These turntables made a terrible clatter as trains passed over each of them in sequence.

Since Derby was an 'open' station, trains from the north and west were halted at low ticket platforms situated respectively on the Five Arches bridge and beneath the London Road bridge for the examination of passenger's tickets. Perhaps it was in consequence of the accident when one Robert Bartlett, the tall policeman who looked after the station front and who, returning late from Nottingham one night, got out of the train at the Five Arches ticket platform and fell into the Derwent from which he was fortunately rescued, that on 16 October 1866 the MR Board ordered the parapets of the bridge be protected by iron railings by the side of the ticket platforms at that location.

On 4 April 1854, the Chairmen's Committee ordered Mr Barlow to furnish an estimate for a carriage shed at the station and it was agreed on 4 July 1854, that a shed for 100 carriages be erected at a cost not exceeding £1,000.

So far as Derby station accommodation was concerned additions were made in the early 1850s to provide, at platform level, a new booking hall for passengers and parcels, together with a 1st class refreshment room, separate waiting rooms for Ladies and Gentlemen and numerous offices for the Director, Secretary, Manager, Superintendent and Clerks, whilst the basement afforded a 2nd class refreshment room, larders, kitchens, ale and wine cellars and compartments for coal, stores and other conveniences.

In October 1856 the foundation stone was laid for a new two-storey block providing for the first time a separate Shareholder's Room. This new block, attached to the station buildings and adjacent to the 1st class booking hall was brought into use the following year and comprised a Shareholders Room 65ft × 40ft × 23ft high lit by eight windows and two fanlights and having a raised platform at one end for the directors with an ante-room. Ground floor accommodation included a boiler room, reading room, library and two class rooms used for many years by the members of the Railway Institute until the latter's new premises opened in 1894 after which they became the home of the Railway Veterans Club. The end of this building is now obscured by a three-storey block added during later alterations.

The MR shareholders originally had to cross

Above:
The MR's fire brigade which covered the Derby area is seen here in 1919 with their Merryweather portable fire engine. *MR Official, Author's Collection*

the main line at the north end of the station to gain access to the former MCR engine shed where meetings were held, but after a fatality when one person was killed while crossing the tracks the meetings were, for a time, transferred to the ground floor of the Cheese Warehouse until 1857 when the new premises were ready.

A corresponding wing was built at the east end of the main entrance in 1857-8 by the same builder, George Thompson.

W. H. Smith & Son had established a bookstall on Derby station at least by 1859 and Mr J. Gallop was its manager for 45 years. He died on 29 August 1904 aged 71 years and during his business career had known and conversed with most of the celebrities of the time.

A drawing for covering in the front entrance to the station at Derby was submitted to the Chairmen's Committee on 6 February 1855 by Mr Lewis and it was agreed that he and Mr Barlow arrange to carry out this at a cost of £259. This 'porte cochère' was subsequently re-sited in front of the new booking hall and office block which was added in 1892.

Mr Lewis was back with a request for further extensive modifications to the station, 'involving considerable expense' on 19 January 1858 and a sub-committee comprising Messrs Paget, Hutchinson, Lewis and Sir Isaac Morley were ordered to consider the question as to the erection of additional buildings and a general re-arrangement of the station accommodation both for traffic and offices'.

No less a personage than Sir Joseph Paxton was added to this 'Derby Station Improvements Committee' on 2 June 1858 and on the following 7 July it was ordered that 'the plan now produced for the proposed alterations and improvement of the station buildings at Derby be carried out as soon as convenient with such modifications as a minute inspection the Committee may think advisable'. Alterations and additional offices costing £2,195 were agreed to on 5 April 1859 and on 6 September further additions were approved at a cost of £1,200.

A new Cheese Warehouse was built at the north end of Derby station early in 1863, John Wood of Derby being paid £2,862 for his work. However, on 18 June 1868, this warehouse, belonging to Smith, Cox & Co, was burned to the ground and over 200 tons of cheese destroyed in a blaze which did some £20,000 worth of damage.

Following this event the MR decided they should set up their own fire brigade. They employed William Medcalf, formerly of the Metropolitan Fire Brigade, to be their new Superintendent from October of the same year and invested in a new Shand-Mason fire engine at a cost of £500. Mounted on a four-wheeled truck, it served the company well until replaced in 1873 by one of a better design by Merryweather's. In addition to the fire engine a new extended system of water mains and hydrants was laid throughout the Works.

On 4 June 1867 the Chairmen's Committee gave final approval to the alteration of the station platforms, etc, at a cost of £2,500. The work included taking out existing turntables to enable a new island platform to be constructed, work undertaken by Edward Dusautoy, a Derby builder of Summerhill, Victoria Street at a cost of £702/6s/5d. He supplied a staircase for the new platform and also constructed the approaches to it whilst Eastwood Swingler & Co and Andrew Handysides of Derby both supplied ironwork for the new facility, whose total cost was £2,661/2s/6d including the necessary permanent way, ballasting and the provision of new signals.

The other set of platforms comprising Nos 4 and 6 with a single line bay platform No 5, giving access to trains from both sides, at the south end, were brought into use in June 1881 in time for the Royal Agricultural Show held in Derby that year. In addition to the platforms a new footbridge was built to connect all six, new hydraulic luggage lifts and additional waiting rooms were provided, and a new length of awning was built over platform 6 which lay outside the original train-shed curtain wall.

As a matter of record, block signalling was established between Derby and Nottingham in December 1869.

Traffic arrangements in the approaches to Derby station from the north and west were much eased by the construction of the relief lines and additional sidings in the locomotive depot. Approval was given by the General Purposes Committee on 31 January 1871 to double the track between Derby North Junction and St Mary's Bridge at a cost of £11,780 and on 4 April 1871 to carry out widening on the 'west branch' (ie: the line to Birmingham) from the Victoria Foundry to London Road at a cost of £7,500 and also to continue the widening to Melbourne Junction at an estimated additional cost of £500. Approval was given on 6 June 1871 to expend a further £1,000 on improving the sidings for locomotives at Derby.

On 3 October 1871 approval was given for the erection of a new block of offices for the MR's Accountant and his staff at a cost of £11,333 and on 3 September 1872 the erection of a new block of offices for the Goods Manager and his staff was agreed at a cost of £19,000. The cost of both was to be charged to capital and they were built on land between Nelson Street and Hulland Street occupying the space between the Midland Hotel and the St Andrew's Goods Wharf of the LNWR. The buildings still stand today occupied mainly by the Regional Mechanical & Electrical Engineer (LMR) and his staff, locally known as 'Nelson Street.'

On 2 January 1872, the GP Committee was informed that Messrs Ellis and Lloyd had finally approved plans for a new Board Room to be built at the station at a cost of £10,800 and on 2 December, 1873 Messrs Gillow & Co had their designs for the decoration of the new room, at an estimated cost of £2,000, accepted.

At the north end of the station on Siddals Road an enginemen's lodging house was constructed in 1872 and the following year a house was built adjacent to it at a cost of £257. These lodgings, consisting of simple dormitories with a dining room, washroom and toilets, were provided in many of the main towns served by the MR and provided overnight accommodation for footplate staff on lodging turns, ie those requiring a night away from home between an outward and a return working.

At the north end of the station, just beyond the Five Arches bridge carrying the tracks over the Derwent, the MR established its own

Above:
The MR's enginemen's lodging-house built in 1872 on the Siddals Road near to the north end of the station and used by men on over-night turns of duty. *Author*

signal works in 1872 on a site between the river and the down main line. Here all the MR's signalboxes (built in sections called 'Flakes') frames, block signalling instruments, bells, repeaters, signals and signal posts were made. The tallest posts measured 65ft in length, of which 6ft was buried in the ground, and were supported by wire guys. Standard posts were 45 or 50ft long.

By the 1880s the original dozen or so carpenters, fitters and smiths had grown into a department of some 500 men at Derby with another 300 elsewhere on the MR system in a total Signal Department comprising some 20

Below:
Interior of the machine and assembly shop of the MR's signal works at Derby on 7 July 1927 showing signalbox lever frames being assembled prior to being dismantled for transportation and installation at the relevant site on the company's system. *G. Waite Collection*

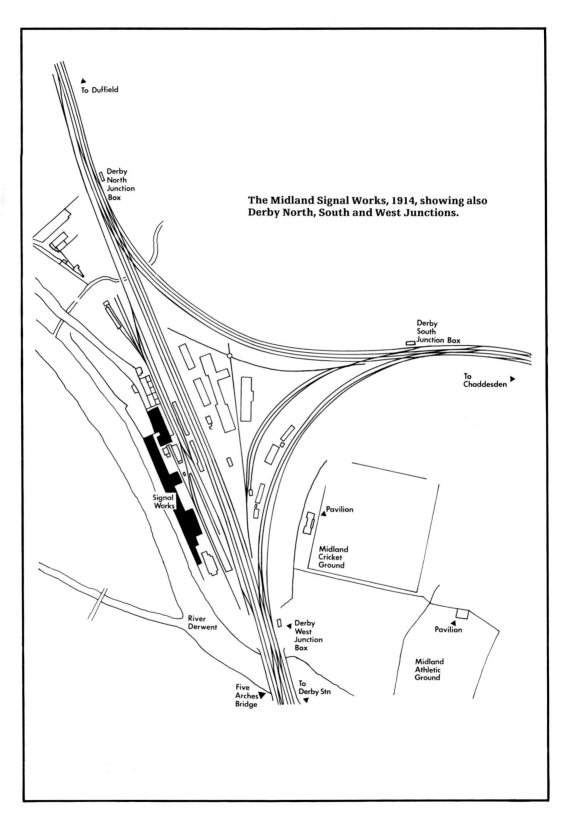

The Midland Signal Works, 1914, showing also Derby North, South and West Junctions.

To Duffield

Derby North Junction Box

Derby South Junction Box

To Chaddesden

Signal Works

Pavilion

Midland Cricket Ground

Pavilion

River Derwent

Derby West Junction Box

Midland Athletic Ground

Five Arches Bridge

To Derby Stn

Above:
The MR's signal works at Derby seen across the River Derwent with the 'Five Arches' bridge and Derby station off to the right. *G. Waite Collection*

districts each with an inspector and 15 to 20 assistants.

A narrow gauge system operated within the shops conveying the heavy posts and equipment from place to place and a branch, which passed beneath the main line, connected the Works with the land in the triangle of lines formed by Derby Junction and Derby North and Derby South Junctions, an area later used for the expansion of the Works in the 1880s, a set of sidings being laid accessed by connections from Derby South Junction.

The Works was modernised in 1912 and continued in operation until 1932 when under LMS auspices the 12,000 items of stock, patterns and machinery were transferred to Crewe. In addition to signalling requirements for the Midland Division of the LMS, the Works also manufactured goods cranes, hoists, lifts, bridge parts, field gates, lifting tackle, wagon traversers and was also responsible for repairs to the company's dredgers.

The network and traffic develops

Returning to the development of lines, the MR's gradual march on Manchester continued with the opening of a new section of line from Rowsley as far as Hassop on 1 August 1862, the railway taking a new alignment by swinging towards the west with a new station at Rowsley, services extending to Buxton on 1 June 1863 and on 1 October 1866 goods trains began running via Chinley and on to the Marple, New Mills and Hayfield Junction Railway at New Mills Junction and thence to Manchester London Road. Passenger opening was delayed by a landslip at Bugsworth and services did not actually commence until 1 February 1867, three months later than planned, goods services having recommenced on 24 January. A more direct route to Manchester London Road opened on 1 August 1875 for passenger traffic and 17 May 1875 for goods, whilst the new direct MR through route

to Manchester Central station via Cheadle Heath opened for passenger traffic on 1 July 1902 and for goods on 5 May 1902, although the MR's London-Manchester passenger services had been using the Central station since 1 January 1880, by running via Stockport Tiviot Dale.

With the opening in 1875 of the new through route from Manchester and Liverpool and the large amount of goods traffic being generated, the pressure on Derby already considerably stretched by the increased number of passenger trains it had to handle, caused the MR Board to promote and construct two relatively short pieces of line to ease the situation. A 6½-mile section of new double track main line was built, linking the old NMR line just north of Ambergate with the Erewash Valley line at

Below:
Webb 2-4-2T No 199 (later LMS No 6608) stands on the turntable outside the L&NWR's shed at Derby in the summer of 1910.
Roger Carpenter Collection

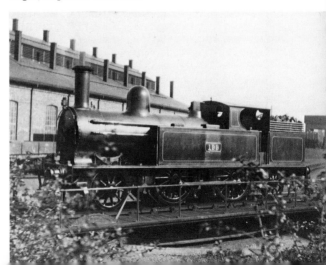

Above:
Midland Railway poster, 1860.

Codnor Park Junction, opened for goods traffic on 1 February 1875 and the following 1 May for passengers, the same date upon which another link line between Trowell and Radford came into use. Thus Derby and Nottingham were afforded better links to Lancashire and the West Riding for both coal and manufacturing goods.

Interestingly, it was at this time that the MR introduced luncheon baskets at Derby station refreshment room and at the Midland Hotel from 1 March 1875 to sustain travellers during their now longer journeys. For three shillings a basket containing half a chicken with ham or tongue, salad, bread, cheese, butter and a half bottle of Claret or Burgundy, could be purchased whilst for two shillings the basket contained veal and ham pie with salad, bread, cheese, butter and a bottle of stout. William Towle, Manager of the Midland Hotel at Derby, who was resposible for this service later went on to become the MR's Hotels Manager.

The opening of the MR's new Settle-Carlisle line on 1 May 1876 for passenger traffic and from 3 August 1875 for goods traffic added new trains to Scotland to the services already calling at Derby and the MR's Pullman cars began using the line, providing both sleeping car and parlour car services. The night sleeper from St Pancras at 9.15pm left Derby at 11.55pm the Edinburgh portion reaching Carlisle at 4.55am and the Scottish capital at 7.35am. The Glasgow portion, having been detached at Skipton, ran non-stop to Carlisle and reached Glasgow (St Enoch) station at 8.00am. The daytime drawing room or 'parlour car' express reached Derby from St Pancras in 2hr 30min and left for Carlisle at 1pm reaching there at 6.18pm and Edinburgh at 9.15pm, while the Glasgow portion, running behind from Skipton by some 12min, reached its destination at 9.20pm via the G&SWR route.

The MR's first dining cars were the *Delmonico* and the *Windsor* converted from the old Pullman cars *Leo* and *Britannia* at Derby in April and July 1882 respectively.

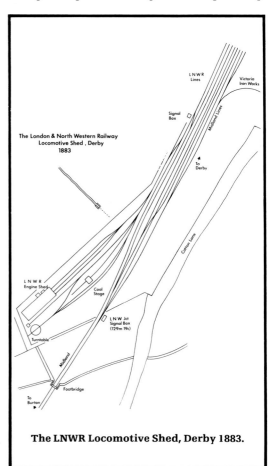

The London & North Western Railway
Locomotive Shed , Derby
1883

The LNWR Locomotive Shed, Derby 1883.

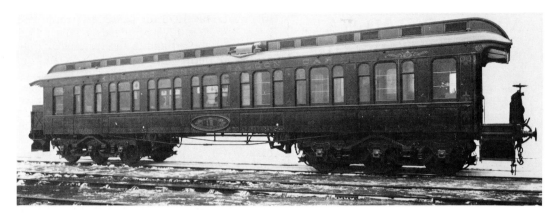

They were introduced on the St Pancras to Manchester expresses on 10 July 1882 and were so successful that following purchase of all parlour cars in October 1883, other conversions followed. However, from 1 July 1884 the Derby stop was omitted and these trains ran via Chaddesden.

In 1888 to counter GNR and LNWR opposition on the routes to Scotland the MR accelerated its 'Scotch' services (as they always referred to them) with faster trains, one of which, the 9.30am from Bristol with through carriages for Edinburgh and Glasgow, reached Derby in just 2hr, with a detour via Camp Hill to prevent passengers transfering to the rival LNWR line at Birmingham thus capturing them for the whole trip!

New competition for the Midland — the Great Northern arrives

The town of Derby was, at this time, still almost exclusively MR territory, given the limited access facilities and services of the NSR and L&NWR companies who shared Derby station, although the latter company had established its own goods shed at St Andrew's at the south end of the station on the northern side of the Birmingham line. A large goods warehouse with six rail tracks had been provided with an external fan of sidings and a series of wagon turntables with a connecting line running laterally across the main tracks, providing a flexible layout within the goods yard itself. The L&NWR company had its own agents at the goods station, at the main station and also in the town at 13 Cornmarket. In 1886 Henry Booth was both agent and stationmaster and James Walton the goods agent.

It also had its own three road engine shed at the side of the line to Birmingham, built in the 1860s just north of Peartree & Normanton station.

Above:
Midland Pullman six-wheeled bogied dining saloon No 15, formerly 'Windsor' and originally 'Britannia', assembled in the Pullman shops at Derby and put into service as a parlour car on 1 June 1874. The conversion to a dining car and from four to six wheeled bogies was done at Derby in July 1882.
MR Official, Crown Copyright courtesy National Railway Museum

Below:
The L&NWR goods warehouse at Derby, now out of use and threatened with demolition. *Author*

The L&NWR began running its own goods trains into the Derby depot from 1 July, 1871 and the NSR company began using the depot for its own goods trains from 1 January 1872. L&NWR passenger trains began running into Derby on a separate service from 1 March 1872.

The NSR also had its own running shed at Derby, the MR Board having been asked in October 1849 to provide 'engine room accommodation'. By 14 January 1851 the Midland Locomotive Committee were recording a proposal to construct a new round house for their own use, noting that 'the NSR company occupy the Birmingham & Derby Shed'.

When the access lines to the new Carriage &

Above:
Derby Locomotive Works with the station on the left before the erection of No 4 shed, circa 1890. The engine is Johnson 4-4-0 No 1320, the NSR locomotive shed is in the left foreground and the Pullman Co car shops are to the right.
MR Official, Author's Collection

Wagon Works were being installed about 1873 this shed stood in the way and was accordingly demolished and a new two road shed erected and it was certainly in use by 1880. Later alterations included a 50ft turntable by Eastwood Swingler & Co in 1895, replacing an earlier 46ft table. The shed usually housed a pair of NSR 0-6-0 goods engines and in later days a 'K' class 4-4-2T engine, and Ahrons records that between 1882 and 1894 three 2-4-0s Nos 7, 10, and 71 were stationed there to work stopping trains to Stoke and Crewe. By January 1918 it had an allocation of nine locomotives.

The shed 'closed' after grouping on 30 June 1923 but locomotives used the site even after demolition of the shed, its two pits, turntable and water column surviving, and became the stabling point for engines working Derby-Crewe stopping trains and some freight trains, including engines being run-in after a visit to Crewe Works.

A circular of 31 December 1925 records 18 men including a foreman allocated to the NSR shed and two engines. In later years, fitters were usually sent across from Derby No 4 Shed to carry out any necessary repairs. The site continued in use until the end of steam working and the arrival of diesel railcar units on the Derby-Crewe services, and subsequently the area was cleared to permit preparations for the erection of Derby Power signalling box, which became operational on 14 July 1969.

As a matter of interest it is worth recording that when the NSR works at Stoke closed on 31 December 1926, staff were transferred to Derby and Crewe, the drawing office staff coming to Derby.

However, on 28 January 1878 another rival entered the town with the opening of a new extension of the GNR for goods traffic, the line serving Ilkeston, West Hallam, Breadsall, Derby, Mickleover and Etwall and joining the

Below:
NSR Adam's 4-4-2T No 46 (later LMS 2182) stands at No 6 platform at Derby with a local train for Stoke-on-Trent on 24 August 1920.
H. C. Casserley

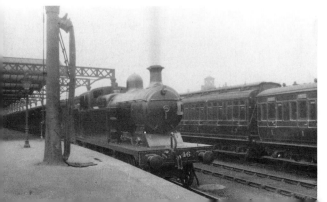

NSR line at Egginton Junction. The opening for passenger services took place on 1 April 1878 with the 9am train from the new Derby station in Friargate to Nottingham London Road, the return train running right through, beyond Derby, to Tutbury from where, after a short stop for refreshment, a return was made to Derby at 12.55am.

This line was promoted to enable the GNR to gain access to collieries in the Notts and Derby coalfield, the most westerly of which were at West Hallam, with an extension to Derby where not only was a four platform station built but also a large three-storey warehouse to be used as a bonded store, grain store and for general goods purposes.

A goods yard with a separate cattle station to deal with livestock were established alongside Dog Kennel Lane (later renamed Great Northern Road) together with a four road locomotive shed complete with a water tower and a 44ft 6in turntable situated on Slack Lane beyond the Old Uttoxeter Road Bridge.

This railway was authorised by the GNR's 'Derbyshire & Staffordshire Extension Bill' which received Royal Assent on 25 July 1872 and in addition to coal traffic the GNR expected to convey not only passengers but also ale from Burton-on-Trent, by virtue of working arrangements with the NSR, manu-factured goods, livestock, and milk from the furthest point of the new extension at Stafford Town. The line also gave the NSR a new route

Above:
A general view of the site of the NSR shed at Derby showing the turntable and water-tower. A three-car diesel railcar unit stands on one of the former shed roads awaiting its return working to Crewe on 25 May 1959. *R. C. Riley*

Below:
The GNR station at Mickleover (for Radbourn) looking towards Derby. The platforms no longer exist and the station buildings form a private dwelling. *B. Lund, Author's Collection*

for long distance passenger and goods traffic into and beyond the East Midlands and was thus relieved of some of its former frustrations at the hands of the MR.

The local firm of Benton & Woodiwiss carried out the building contract at a tendered price of £2,408,299 for the 40½ miles of railway, which included expensive high via-ducts and bridges and a large amount of earthworks and which occupied the contrac-tors for almost six years.

Above:
The former GNR locomotive shed at Slack Lane, Derby in early BR days on 21 September 1952. Engines on shed were 'J5' No 65498 (outside), 'J39' No 64747, 'J2' No 65022, 'J6' No 64213, 'J50' No 68982 and 'J5' No 65490. *R. J. Buckley*

The new station at Derby Friargate, with a fine bridge over that throughfare faced by attractive arched cast iron decorated panels detached from the main load bearing members of the bridge and manufactured by the famous Andrew Handyside & Co of Duke Street, Derby, was more conveniently situated to the town centre than the Midland station, and comprised a main island platform approached by means of a subway running transversely beneath the lines with a booking office at that level on the north side. A pair of outside platforms was provided but they were mainly used for excursion traffic although the tracks

Below:
The 11.00am special from Derby Friargate to Skegness heads past the closed ex-GNR Derby Racecourse station on 19 April 1954 hauled by ex-LNER Class B1 4-6-0 No 61192. *R. J. Buckley*

were used as through goods lines when the inner lines were occupied.

To the east of the station the railway ran along a series of arches, 11 in all including those upon which the station was built, and reached the Duke Street branch which curved away on the north side to serve various sidings and a branch of the Derby Canal alongside the River Derwent, whilst beyond the river another connection ran down to Derby Racecourse siding which served that establishment from the 1890s until its closure about 1938.

Beyond Derby Friargate station to the east on the GNR's line lay Breadsall station, serving that charming village some two miles from Derby (fare in 1894 2d 2nd and 4d 1st class), whilst to the west Mickleover for Radbourne (2½ miles, fares 2½d and 5d) and Etwall stations (6 miles, fares 6d and 10d) served those villages, the stations being well constructed in pleasing red brick.

In 1880 eight weekday passenger trains ran each way between Burton and Nottingham, the first of the day at 6.20am running only between Derby and Burton. Seven up goods (three only on Mondays) and eight down completed the services through Derby with an extra down goods on Wednesdays and Saturdays only.

By 1883 Derby services had been increased to 10 passenger trains in each direction of which six each way ran from and to Stafford, and a weekday service between Burton and Egginton Junction had been introduced with four 'up' and five 'down' trains daily.

On 21 August 1896 an agreement was made between the GNR and NSR companies affording reciprocal running powers to the GNR to work through goods traffic between Colwick and Alsager and between Peterborough and Boston to Stoke-on-Trent, the NSR being permitted, in return, to work between Alsager and Colwick.

Goods traffic had increased with nine trains each way serving Burton, Retford, Nottingham, Doncaster, Colwick, Ratcliffe-on-Trent and London King's Cross.

A new joint LD&ECR and GNR station, Nottingham Victoria, was opened on 24 May 1900 and trains from Burton and Stafford were extended beyond Nottingham to service Newark and Grantham.

The GNR developed holiday traffic to both the east and west coasts, the *Derby Mercury* of 16 July, 1909 advertising 'Holidays on the East Coast — Restaurant Car Express Service via the GNR' with through bookings via the Midland & Great Northern Railway to Sheringham, Cromer, Great Yarmouth and Lowestoft at 13 shillings return. That same summer the GNR linked with the North Stafford to provide daily through trains to North Wales resorts

Above:
Handysides' fine bridge over Friargate, Derby built in 1878 to carry the GNR line into their station to the right. *Author*

with GNR coaches being attached to NSR trains at Uttoxeter or Tutbury. These services continued up to World War 1 when they were suspended and not reinstated for another 40 years.

Ordinary train services remained unaffected by World War 1 until 1 January 1917, when they were drastically reduced. A total of five trains between Burton and Derby and four between Stafford and Derby disappeared. By 20 October 1922, Derby Friargate was served by 11 trains on each branch.

By this same date 14 up and 17 down goods trains were passing through Derby, the traffic

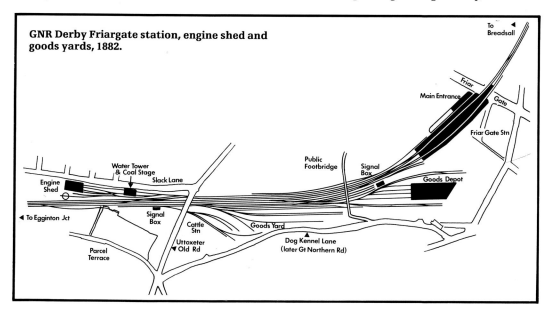

GNR Derby Friargate station, engine shed and goods yards, 1882.

Above:
The large GNR warehouse at Friargate, Derby still in use in September 1985 for other than railway purposes, although the basement was by then sealed off. *Author*

comprising ale en route from Burton to Newcastle, livestock for Spitalfields Market, milk (as much as 1,700gal daily from Grindley alone) to King's Cross from Staffordshire which also supplied some local Derby needs.

Eastbound traffic was routed via Colwick with some via Leen Valley Junction or Bulwell Common, and that for the west at Burton, Stafford or Egginton Junction.

A little way from Friargate station on the Ashbourne Road the Railway Servants Orphanage was established in 1875 to provide a home for up to 150 children of railway servants killed whilst on duty. A new brick building with stone dressings and standing in four acres of ground was opened in 1887 which increased accommodation to provide for 300 children. The orphanage, which formed a department of the Railway Benevolent Institution, was supported by all of the railway companies in the country and depended entirely on voluntary contributions.

Returning to MR matters, in 1877 Derby Corporation took Litchurch, where the MR premises were mainly situated, into the borough, the township by then occupying an area greater than that of Derby itself before the railways had arrived!

Reviewing MR train services — by August 1887 Derby was being served by no less than 78 trains during weekdays. The 'Pullman' sleeper called at 3.37am on its way from St Pancras to Manchester and Liverpool and a 'Pullman' parlour car express left for Manchester at 1.9pm arriving there at 2.35 whilst at 1.15pm an express for Manchester, with through carriages for Liverpool, departed. In mid-afternoon the 'Pullman' parlour car express, 12 noon from St Pancras, left at 3.05pm reaching its destination in 2hr 5min. Three special London expresses for Manches-

Below:
Period view of the North end of Derby Midland station looking towards the Locomotive Works about 1888. *MR Official, Author's Collection*

ter Central avoided Derby station and ran via Chaddesden. Other expresses for Manchester and Liverpool departed at 6.40pm ('Pullman' parlour) 7.57pm (Dining Saloon car) and there was a 12.30pm overnight train to Liverpool and Manchester. Other trains to Manchester departed at 7.15am (slow) 8.15am (express arriving 10am), 10.23 (12.35pm), 3.50 (slow 5.45, and to Liverpool 6.35). Trains for Buxton left at 9.28am (slow), 12.30pm (fast arr. 1.52) 1.35pm (slow), 5.30pm (slow) and 6.55pm (slow), and a slow train left for Bakewell at 8.30pm.

Services via Leeds to Carlisle and beyond over the Settle and Carlisle line left Derby at 10.15pm ('Pullman' sleeper — Carlisle 3.26am, Edinburgh 5.53am and Glasgow 6.20am); 11.48pm (Carlisle 4.30am Edinburgh 7.25am and Glasgow 7.40am); 3.27am (Carlisle 10.17am); 7.40am (Carlisle 1.38pm, Edinburgh 4.32pm, Glasgow 4.37pm), 11.45am, 1.25pm 'Pullman' parlour (Carlisle 6.05pm, Edinburgh 8.42pm Glasgow 8.55pm); and 1.40pm (Carlisle 8.05pm, Edinburgh 10.37pm Glasgow 11.40pm).

Trains to Birmingham, Gloucester and Bristol, with a best time to the latter of 3hr 20min, left Derby at 12.35am (Mail), 1.58am (through 'Scotch' express from Edinburgh and Glasgow, MX) 6.20am (local to Birmingham), 6.40 (semi-fast), 8.47 (slow to Bristol and Gloucester), 10.30 (express), 10.40 (slow), 11.40 (express), 1.20pm (local to Birmingham), 2.5pm (through express from Newcastle and York), 2.30pm (local to Burton), 3.45pm (semi-fast), 5.10pm (local to Burton), 5.35pm (local to Birmingham), 6.35pm (local to Burton), 7.10pm (express), 9pm and 9.45pm (locals to Birmingham). There was also a through carriage working, begun in 1880, between Bradford and Bournemouth via the S&DJR and another through coach service between Bradford and Plymouth (Friary) via Templecombe and the L&SWR.

In the Sheffield direction there was a variety of local trains with expresses to Leeds at 7.40am, 1.25pm, 2.55pm, 3.55pm, 6.47pm, 8.15pm, 12.45am and 3.27am.

There was also a good variety of purely local services, the Ripley branch having a service of four trains to and from Derby as did the Wirksworth branch, the Ashby route and also the service from Derby to Nottingham which ran via Castle Donington. Most intensive was the local service between Derby and Nottingham with 28 trains from and 30 to Derby.

Trains for St Pancras and points in between left Derby at 6am (arrived 10.30am), 7.05am (to Loughborough), 8.45am (11.50am), 10.07am (to

Leicester), 9.27am (via Nottingham and Kettering, due at 12.55 in St Pancras), 11.41am ('Pullman' parlour car, arrived 2.35pm), 12.15pm (to Leicester), 1.15pm ('Pullman' parlour car from Liverpool arrived 4.15), 2.47pm ('Pullman' parlour car from Manchester, arrived 5.40), 3.40pm (arrive 7.15), 4.20 and 5.27pm (to Leicester), 5.15pm (London Express combining with 'Pullman' parlour car express from Manchester at Leicester and arriving St Pancras 8.15), 6.50pm (Dining Saloon car train from Manchester, arriving 9.40), 6.54pm (to Leicester) 9.25pm (arriving 2.20am) 12.50am (due St Pancras 4.15am), 1.57am (arriving 5.15am).

The MR express trains were by now hauled by the new standard 4-4-0 type locomotive but in June 1887, the first of Johnson's single driving-wheeled 4-2-2 express engines, No 25, emerged from Derby Works, a total of 95 of this type being constructed between then and 1900 to work fast light expresses over MR lines between Derby/Nottingham and Liverpool, London and Leeds, and from 1892 they were introduced on the Bristol services.

The NSR main line from Derby to Crewe provided a regular service with a short cross-country link service from Burton-on-Trent via Horninglow joining the main line at Tutbury, these trains being known locally as the 'Tutbury Jinny'. Trains left Derby for Stoke-on-Trent and Crewe at 8.0am (terminating at Harecastle, for the Audley branch), 8.50am (arrive Crewe 10.30), 11.00am (arrive 12.40), 1.55pm (arrive 3.42), 2.35pm (Saturdays only to Uttoxeter), 4.20pm (arrive 6.45) and 7pm (arrive 8.58pm). Uttoxeter was the interchange point for a route via the Churnet

Above:

The 'south' end of Derby Midland station about 1912 as an express leaves for Stoke-on-Trent in the care of 2-4-0 No 54. *Author's Collection*

Valley for the 32 miles to Macclesfield, with an overall time from Derby of 2hr 20min. The NSR trains which penetrated deepest into foreign territory included the summer through expresses from Nottingham and Derby to Llandudno which ran more miles over other companies lines than over their own.

Below:

Midland Class 3P 4-4-0 No 763 heading towards Derby through Pear Tree & Normanton station with a mixed train about 1925. Note the ticket office by the bridge.

L&GRP courtesy David & Charles/V. Forster

L&NWR services from Derby ran via Burton-on-Trent and Lichfield to Walsall with connections from there to Birmingham, Wolverhampton, Wednesbury and Dudley, there being nine trains each way on weekdays. From 1 May 1885, the L&NWR introduced a new express service between Derby and Birmingham with connections at Burton for Uttoxeter and the Crewe line.

Perhaps the most intense activity at Derby station occurred during the mass exodus of workers from 'the Loco and Carriage side' (as they are colloquially referred to) once each year on the occasion of the annual Works holiday. From the early morning trains were departing for all the most popular destinations such as Skegness, Blackpool and the North Wales resorts — each train dutifully seen off from the station by the Works Manager (or a Foreman as his representative), at whatever the hour — and some of the trains left around 4.30am!

Another important and regular traffic at Derby station in the 1880s was that of milk sent in by farmers from the rich meadowland around Duffield, Wirksworth and Castle Donington for, with charges of only a ½d a gallon for short distances and 1d for long distance carriage, it was well worthwhile to send the milk to distant towns and cities via the Midland. Arriving by the earliest morning local trains the milk would be collected on the centre platforms at Derby for transportation by the 8am morning milk train comprising as many as 10 vans each with 40 churns holding 15gal apiece. Similar arrangements were made for the evening traffic and continued until the 1920s when the establishment of local co-operative dairies and bottling plants served by road motor transport, caused its gradual demise.

In the days before the cinema there were many travelling theatre companies and most Sundays were taken up by moving on to a new venue. As an important junction, Derby was the great meeting-place of the profession as Cicely Hamilton recalls. 'I always liked a Sunday wait at Derby, where every train had its labelled theatrical carriages and where theatrical specials were shunted, assembled and divided. As each train came up you hurried to read its labels and call on any member of the company with whom you had previous acquaintance!'

Turning to goods traffic, St Mary's Yard had developed over the years and its use extended to handling a large range of manufactured goods of all kinds, along with raw materials and partly finished goods. Heavy train loads of items such as bridge sections and other fabricated steelwork were handled here and a bonded stores facility was provided as was usual at the larger MR goods depots. A new Fish shed was completed by George Walker-dine, Builder, in August 1882 and the following year a new horse dock was added.

Chaddesden Sidings, in reality a chain of three eventual marshalling yards extending along the north east side of the former MCR line from Derby to Nottingham, was established both as a handling yard for local traffic and for re-marshalling freight and mineral trains arriving along the main artery routes. After 1875 Derby was largely avoided by the bulk of coal traffic, since most travelled from the Notts and Derby coalfield either along the Erewash Valley line using the Butterley route

Above:
St Mary's goods yard on 26 June 1911 as a pair of hand cranes are used to carefully load a 'Silver Ghost' chassis from the Rolls-Royce works in the town. *Derby Museums*

into Lancashire and the West Riding of Yorkshire, via Trent to London, or to Birmingham and the west over the Sheet Stores Junction-Stenson Junction line.

Despite the extensive alterations at St Mary's goods yard and the marshalling yards at Chaddesden the passage of freight traffic through Derby station area was still constricted by the bottleneck at the Five Arches bridge which still had only two tracks passing over it. Accordingly, a contract was

Below:
Transferring a palletised load between a horse-drawn dray and an early motor lorry at Derby in 1917. *MR Official, Author's Collection*

placed with Joseph D. Nowell of Manchester for the erection of an additional width of viaduct over the River Derwent and bridges over the Derby Canal and the road giving access into the Locomotive Works in a widening scheme devised by J. Allen Macdonald, the MR Civil Engineer, at an eventual cost of £15,863/6s/0d. The new arrangements were opened for traffic on 9 October, 1892, formally inspected by Major Marinder of the Railway Inspectorate on 8 January 1893, and given a final certificate in April 1893.

1892 also saw great improvements taking place in the appearance of Derby station. The porte cochère, erected in 1855, was dismantled and a new two-storey block built in front of the old Thompson buildings, stretching between

the shareholders' room to the right and the similar but three-storied block to the left, the shareholders' room having received a matching three-storied fronting block.

Below the first floor offices of the new central block handsome new 1st and 3rd class booking halls were provided with an arrivals hall adjacent to the 3rd class hall. Decorative domed towers, sheeted in lead, were added at each end of the new central block which was topped by a stone balustrade with a central pedimented feature comprising a magnificent clock, set in a decorated stone surround featuring carved Wyverns, the whole being surmounted by a complete Wyvern, the mythical creature which forms the crest of the MR's second armorial device, set on a separate stone pedestal above the clock feature. In front of this new central block a replica of the old porte cochère was erected using some of the old materials to provide glass-covered arrival and departure bays for carriages.

Returning to MR train services — 1893 saw a dramatic slump in revenue of which a major factor was the great coal strike, and train loadings were dramatically reduced. In the middle of September the Traffic Committee withdrew all the Pullman drawing room cars, which represented a high trailing load, from traffic and placed them in store in the carriage

Above:
Baldwin 2-6-0s, brought in kit form from America, being re-erected in the open air in front of the Derby Locomotive Works offices in 1899 during the great locomotive shortage.
MR Official, Author's Collection

shed at Spondon Junction at the southern end of Chaddesden Sidings.

However, the second half of the 1890s witnessed a revival and a tremendous increase in goods traffic throughout Britain and the Derby Locomotive Works was at full stretch providing engines to meet the demand, so much so that in 1898 40 2-6-0s were ordered and imported in kit form from the Baldwin (30) and the Schenectady (10) Works in North America, assembled at Derby (the Baldwin's outdoor!) and all put into service on the MR

Below:
MR Class 3 4-4-0 No 758 apparently making a spirited start from the south end of Derby Midland station about 1912 heading for Bristol; however a carriage door is clearly open towards the rear of the train! *MR Official, Author's Collection*

hauling freight and mineral trains by the end of 1899. They were part of a Government order for one hundred 2-6-0s to be shared between the MR, GNR and GCR companies.

On the passenger front improvements to west services calling at Derby were made by the introduction of three new trains of vehicles for the Bradford, Leeds, Birmingham and Bristol dining car trains each with both 1st and 3rd class 60ft dining carriages all with a 31ft kitchen car, 60ft 3rd class bogie and composite bogie coaches, both with lavatories and a 31ft passenger luggage van, all built at Derby. Hauled by Johnson 4-2-2s these trains were placed in service on 2 August 1897.

In July 1899 a special direct series of trains were introduced by the MR to Southampton in connection with 'American' line sailings to New York and 'Union' and 'Castle' Lines to Capetown, South Africa. These trains ran on Fridays only from Scotland and the North with departure from Derby at 3.15am on Saturday mornings and running via Cheltenham and the Midland & South Western Junction Railway, were due in Southampton at 9.10am in time to catch the boats.

The end of 1900 saw a steady improvement in the speeds of passenger trains over the whole system for up to that time George Henry Turner, General Manager, had held that his great MR system was essentially a 'goods line' and passenger services had suffered accordingly. Turner had succeeded John Noble upon his resignation on ill health grounds in May 1892.

Public opinion had been critical of the MR for considering its shareholders by concentrating on the efficient handling of a great volume of lucrative coal traffic rather than following its competitors by promoting 'catchpenny flights with passenger services like some people', letters even appearing in the press asking 'Is the Midland asleep?'.

However, with Turner's departure the word was to accelerate services and typically the fastest from St Pancras to Kettering at an average speed of 52mph was accelerated to 56¾mph, services to and from Derby similarly benefitting.

In 1903 additional expresses from Derby to the West ran at 10.25am and 12.28pm in connection with trains from York and beyond, whilst a new 7.20pm express from Sheffield provided better journey times between Glasgow (1.30pm) and Leeds (6.20pm) and Bristol. There were also additional trains and reduced journey times on all other routes.

Derby was being served at this time by two dining car trains to Manchester at 6.57pm and

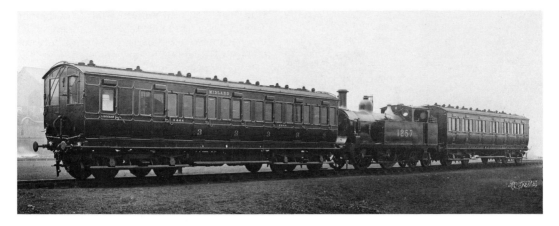

9.25pm and three for London (St Pancras) at 10.47am, 1.38pm and 7.15pm. A northbound 1st class sleeping car train still left Derby at 11.55pm for Edinburgh and Glasgow and the southbound sleeper called at Derby at 2.12am on its way to St Pancras where it arrived at 5.25am, passengers being allowed to stay on board until 8am. Three dining car trains served Derby from Bristol arriving at 3.28pm, 5.28pm and 8.15pm, the second continuing to Bradford arriving there at 7.50pm in an overall time of 5hr 40min. The service in the reverse direction left Bradford at 10.35am arriving at Derby at 12.45pm and Bristol at 3.55pm. The other dining car trains for Bristol left Derby at 10.25am and 6.05pm.

Since the Wirksworth branch had not been extended northwards to form part of a main route to Manchester, its services had remained infrequent with only four each way on weekdays and one each way on Sundays.

However, in response to agitation by the inhabitants of Wirksworth and other 'cul-de-sac' routes, the MR introduced a rail motor service on 1 March 1906 utilising four old Pullman parlour cars and four M&GNJR 4-4-0T locomotives then on loan to the MR. Wirksworth was given two additional weekday services, third class only, from Derby at 8.45am and 1.55pm returning at 9.45am and 2.50pm; the Derby to Melbourne service was improved by three trains leaving Derby at 7.40am, 12.05pm and 4.55pm (FX) and returning at 8.12am, 12.38pm and 5.23pm (FX), whilst the Derby and Ripley service had but one additional train out at 10.32am and returning at 11.25am.

A mention is here necessary of the vital role of the main Control Office at Derby station in monitoring and controlling the movements of goods and mineral trains over the whole of the MR's network of lines. Before the first relief

office was established at Masboro' in July 1907 delays to traffic were considerable and as an example four trains had stood at Treeton a total of 68hr, the longest delayed, behind engine No 1051, having been stationary for no less than 21hr! Some 24,760 MR drivers, firemen and guards were having to remain on duty up to 15 hours or more, so the Midland Train Control system was introduced with the main Control Office at Derby, open day and night and linked to District Offices in every area. The first actual section under control office working was that between Toton and Normanton in January 1909. Reporting stations recorded the passage of trains, identified by coded letters on each goods brake van with codes for each location and the starting time in letters coded A to L (excepting J) to represent 1 to 12 on the clock. By 1912

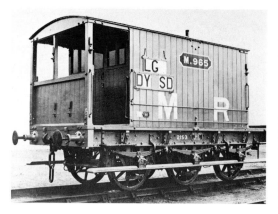

Above:

MR 20 ton goods brake van No 965, built at Derby in 1904 and displaying the Train Control System codes.

MR Official, Midland Railway Trust Collection

Below:

Midland and South Eastern & Chatham through service timetable, 1911.

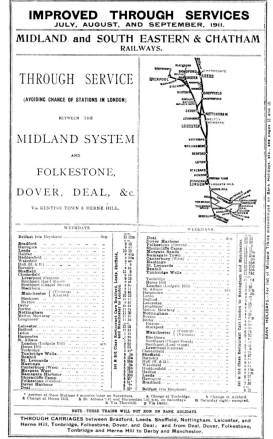

delays were down 87% from 746 to 90, with an almost immediate decrease of over 67% the year after introduction. The average speed of goods trains went up from 4.9mph to 6.3mph and receipts increased by 13.7%.

Staff at Derby HQ Control worked three shifts, with a Controller and Deputy Controller always on duty whilst a third person acted as regulator for the passage of freight trains, passenger working being already well regulated by the working timetable. A system of cards — white for down trains, pink for up trains, blue for drivers and green for guards — recorded details of each vehicle's movements with loadings on the reverse side. Derby's own local control office was at Chaddesden and extended to Stretton in the north, Sheet Stores Junction in the east and Clay Mills in the west. All main signalboxes were linked into the system and signalbox boys were responsible for recording the passage of all train times in the box register. 'Control' was thus able to closely monitor the progress of each train and relieve drivers of delayed trains as required.

Midland through services via Derby in the summer of 1909 included through corridor expresses from Bournemouth and Bath and also from St Pancras through Sheffield and thence via the new MR connection from Royston to Thornhill over the L&Y to Dewsbury, Huddersfield, Halifax and Bradford Exchange.

Another through service, operated jointly by the MR and South Eastern & Chatham Railways, linked Bradford and Manchester (from where a restaurant car ran as far as Hendon) to Folkestone, Dover and Deal.

By 1911 other through services were running via Derby between London and Keswick via Carnforth and Derby had a through carriage service to Bath, Blackpool, Cromer Beach, Dumfries, Edinburgh, Exeter, Glasgow, Heysham, Kingswear, Lowestoft, Newcastle, Perth, Plymouth, Scarborough, Southampton, Torquay, Weston-super-Mare and Yarmouth Beach.

The outbreak of war with Germany on 3 August 1914 had an immediate affect on the MR and all excursion traffic was cancelled with effect from 5 August.

Between 5am on 15 August and 10.30pm on 16 August, no less than 67 special goods trains were marshalled and run from Carlisle to Bedford with a further 65 specials between 7am on 15 August and 1am on 16 August from the Derby and Burton-on-Trent area, in connection with special war requirements.

By 1917 very much reduced public services were being run as a result of the war and passenger traffic through Derby, as elsewhere, was down to almost half its prewar mileages.

Only seven trains ran to London St Pancras, in a best time of 3hr 1min, with eight in the reverse direction, the fastest being the 'Manchester Corridor Express' with restaurant facilities, which left St Pancras at 4.15pm and reached Derby in 2hr 53min. The Manchester, Liverpool and Leeds 'Restaurant Car' express, which ran via Nottingham where it was divided, reached Derby from St Pancras in 3hr 10min, Manchester Central in a further 2hr 10min and Liverpool Central 1hr 20min later.

Through services to the West included the Bradford and Leeds 'Corridor' express reaching Bristol from Derby in 3hr 45min, whilst in the reverse direction three and a half hours was the best time for the trip whilst the 'York Corridor Express' reached Derby from Bristol in 5min less and went on to York in a further 2hr 20min.

As the war continued the MR was called upon not only to supply munitions and ambulance trains but to work a large number of special trains, and stations all over the system dealt with no less than 3,982 ambulance trains conveying almost 340,000 personnel in all.

After World War 1 railways everywhere struggled to regain normality and restore lost services, but road vehicles had made inroads and now presented a great threat to railways in general, the MR being no exception. Between 1904 and 1919 the number of private cars had increased from 8,465 to 109,715 and one year later to 186,801. By 1922 an even greater increase to 314,769 took place, with a trebling of the number of general motor vehicles, whilst the number of goods road vehicles rose from 4,000 in 1904 to 150,995 by 1922, with inevitable consequences to the railways.

In March 1919 the MR began to recover some of its prewar image by restoring some of its best trains including the 10.15am Bristol-Leeds, the 2.05pm St Pancras to Manchester, the 3.15pm Leeds to Bristol and the 4.20pm Manchester Express to London St Pancras. From May 1919 a new timetable appeared with services between St Pancras and Manchester in 4hr 30min and improved services from the West Riding to Bristol.

Derby remodelled its MR main line services in 1921 and many were further accelerated, the journey time between London St Pancras and Manchester Central for instance being dramatically reduced by the fastest trains to 4hr, as exampled by the 10.25 which reached Derby in

Above:
The telegraph office at Derby in 1930 showing operators at work and baskets for the messages labelled 'Euston', 'Crewe', and 'Post Office (No 2)'. Messages could relate not only to railway operating matters but also be personal ones from passengers of delayed trains telegraphed from the next stopping place and relayed to relatives via the GPO. *G. Waite Collection*

Below:
The cattle dock at the Royal Show held on the Osmaston Park, Derby in June 1921. The locomotive is 0-6-0 No 3488. *MR Official, Author's Collection*

2hr 29min and went on to reach Manchester at 2.25pm and Liverpool Central at 3.15pm.

However, the MR empire, centred on Derby, was not only never destined to regain its former pride of place in competition with its rivals, but was to lose its separate identity in the merger of railway companies which took place on 1 January 1923 when the Scottish Railway Co became a part of the new 'London, Midland & Scottish Railway Co', which was to embrace not only former competitors like the L&NWR and the NSR, but also the Lancashire & Yorkshire, Furness, Caledonian, Glasgow & South Western and Highland Railway companies as well as a number of other minor and joint railways. This amalgamation had quite an effect on Derby as a railway centre as we shall see.

Post grouping days (1923-1948)

With a route mileage of 7,790 miles plus a little over 200 in Ireland under the Northern Counties Committee, the new London Midland & Scottish Railway Co was by size the largest in the world, although its route mileage was exceeded by some American companies. It was subdivided into Western, Central, Midland and Northern Divisions for operating purposes and Derby became the location of the Chief General Superintendent's Department controlling the four Divisional offices, at Derby (former MR and subsidiary lines), Crewe (former L&NWR and subsidiaries), Manchester (former L&YR lines) and Glasgow (former Caledonian, Highland and G&SWR lines).

However, the cramped headquarters of the new LMSR was at Euston, with Sir William Guy Granet, the ex-MR chairman as one of two deputies to the First Chairman, Charles Napier Lawrence of the L&NWR, the other being another L&NWR man. Edward Brocklehurst Fielden. The MR had seemingly joined a larger railway network but the key positions of administration lay with the L&NWR and L&YR men. Derby's demise as a headquarters came with the disbanding of the General Super-

Below:
The forecourt of Derby Midland station in September 1921 with an early taxi-cab and horse-drawn cabs waiting for hire. The electric tramcar is for Pear Tree, a Derby suburb and in the left background is the MR Institute.
Author's Collection

Above:
L&NWR 'George the Fifth' class 4-4-0 No 882 *Canada* leaving Derby Midland with an express for Crewe, the type of working to which they were relegated after being re-classified by the LMS in 1924. *Henry J. Salmon*

Below:
LMS excursion leaflet, 1925.

intendents organisation and the opening of Euston House in 1932.

In the early years of the LMS there was some limited acceleration of services to and from Derby, but improvements in services between Manchester and London St Pancras were centred on Nottingham, and Derby's season ticket holders were, for instance, not allowed to use the 8.55am express from Manchester which now began to run via Nottingham, as well as Derby, from where it ran non-stop to St Pancras.

In 1927 the LMS gave titles to a number of trains amongst which was the 'Devonian', an old service consisting of three coaches handed over at Bristol by the GWR and worked through to Bradford Forster Square station. In 1937 the LMS accelerated the train which was booked to leave Paignton at 9.15am and Torquay at 9.22am, taking a leisurely 2hr 58min to reach Bristol where the through coaches were attached to the rear of an LMS restaurant car formation. Leaving Bristol at 12.35pm the train reached Derby at 3.25pm, Leeds at 5.24pm and Bradford at 5.54pm, a total journey time of 8hr 39min from Paignton. From May to September inclusive the entire train of LMS stock plus the restaurant car (in use as far as Bristol) worked through to Kingswear on the River Dart, giving a journey time from Derby of 6hr 32min and on some Saturdays the train ran in several parts.

A variety of through carriages worked to and from Derby, odd examples being that a coach from Bradford was dropped off from the 'Devonian' at Derby, whilst a through Newcastle-Bristol coach, which had come south via the 10.20am ex-York was acquired. For many years the Manchester expresses from St Pancras had left at 25min past alternate hours, commencing at 8.25am, thus

ISSUE.—See subsequent bills for altered train times commencing June 20th.   D 964.

L M S

LONDON MIDLAND AND SCOTTISH RAILWAY

EVERY SATURDAY, Commencing May 2nd, 1925, until June 13th,
(May 30th excepted, for which date see special bills for additional facilities),

COOK'S

EXCURSIONS for 8 or 15 days,
WILL RUN AS UNDER TO

BRIDLINGTON
FILEY, WHITBY, AND
SCARBOROUGH

FROM "Midland" Stations	Times of Starting.	RETURN FARES (Third Class)—to			
		BRIDLINGTON	FILEY	SCARBORO'	WHITBY
		s. d.	s. d.	s. d.	s. d.
Burton-on-Trent ...	p.m. 12.23	21 3	23 0	22 6	25 0
DERBY	12.45	19 6	21 3	20 9	23 0
Belper	a.m. 11.16	18 0	20 0	19 6	22 0
Ambergate	11.42	17 9	19 9	19 0	21 6
Bridlington ...arr.	6.3 p.m.				
Filey "	5.29 "				
Scarboro' (Ordinary Station) "	5.7 "				
Whitby "	7.5 "				

RETURN ARRANGEMENTS.—Passengers return on the Saturday or Saturday Week following date of outward journey, as under—
From WHITBY at 12.5 p.m.   SCARBORO' (Ordinary Station) at 1.10 p.m.   FILEY at 12.47 p.m.
BRIDLINGTON at 12.11 p.m.

CONDITIONS OF ISSUE OF TICKETS.
CHILDREN under three years of age, free ; three years and under twelve, half-fares.
Excursion tickets are not transferable and will be available only to and from the stations named upon them, and by the trains, and on the dates specified on the announcements.
The Company give notice that tickets for excursions are issued at a reduced rate, and subject to the condition that the Company shall not be liable for any loss, damage, injury, or delay to passengers, arising from any cause whatsoever.
Passengers are allowed 100 lbs. of personal luggage free at owner's risk.

PASSENGERS ARE REQUESTED TO OBTAIN TICKETS IN ADVANCE, TO ENABLE THE COMPANY TO PROVIDE SUITABLE ACCOMMODATION FOR THEIR JOURNEY.
TICKETS CAN BE PURCHASED at the "MIDLAND" STATIONS, and at the "MIDLAND" TOWN OFFICE, 17, Corn Market, DERBY.
All information regarding Excursion Trains on the London Midland & Scottish Railway can be obtained on application to Divisional Passenger Commercial Superintendent, New St. Station, Birmingham, and General Superintendent (Passenger Commercial) Derby.

April, 1925.   **H. G. BURGESS, General Manager.**

3d 263/1925.   Thos. Cook & Son, Ltd., Printers, &c., Ludgate Circus, London, E.C.4.   (2/462)

Above:
Spondon station is the first out of Derby on the London line and is to the left of this view showing the large MR signalbox and the level crossing giving access to the British Celanese works beyond as it appeared on 20 November 1924. *LMSR Official, Author's Collection*

Below:
Ex-L&NWR 'Claughton' class 4-6-0 No 5984 at the head of a Derby to Leeds train passing Duffield about 1934. *The late F. G. Carrier*

earning the nickname of the 'Twenty-Fives' but from 27 September 1937 these were retimed to start at 30min past the alternate hours and in the following year the LMS bestowed the names the 'Peak Express' to the 10.30am down and the 'Palatine' to the 4.30pm, the up trains with these names leaving respectively at 4.25pm and 10am from Manchester Central. From the 1937 accelerations, the down 'Peak Express' ran between St Pan-

cras and Manchester in 3hr 35min which restored a journey time from MR days.

However, in 1939 this train was slowed by 21min caused by the insertion of four additional stops between Derby and Manchester, and a through coach provided for Liverpool. Stanier 4-6-0s were responsible for faster timings, with seven-coach trains as far as Chinley, where the Liverpool coach was detached, and six coaches onwards to Manchester.

The 1937 accelerations came as a result of dynamometer car tests in April of that year. Light train loadings coupled with the raising of maximum permitted speeds through curves such as those at Ambergate and Trent enabled thirty start to stop runs on the Midland Division to run at average speeds of 60mph and over. As an example on the St Pancras to Manchester services 'down' trains were accelerated by up to 40min, the best being the 10.30am whilst the best saving by an 'up' train from Manchester was 42min by the 6.20pm departure.

Other through services via Derby included carriages from Edinburgh and Glasgow to Bristol, and a Nottingham-Bristol express which ran via Chaddesden and left Derby at 8.22am reaching Bristol 11.36am. There was also a through express service on Saturdays only to and from Blackpool (North), and even Burton-on-Trent could boast of a through London express leaving at 10am via Derby (10.15) and arriving at St Pancras at 4.30pm.

There was a vast number of through carriage services passing through Derby, many with a restaurant car service for the whole or part of the journey and the 6.06pm departure from Derby to Birmingham offered both teas and 'a la carte' meals during the journey of 1hr 9min — a pleasant relaxation after a day's business and a boon to hard pressed railway officers! This train had originated at Hull leaving at 2.05pm, its final destination being Worcester.

Through carriages also operated from Derby to Bath, Bournemouth West, Edinburgh Waverley, Exeter, Glasgow St Enoch, Llandudno, Lowestoft, Manchester Victoria, Newcastle-on-Tyne, Paignton, Scarborough, Taunton, Torquay, Weston-super-Mare and Yarmouth Beach and these were additional to the through services of complete trains, being detached and worked forward to their destinations at appropriate points in the journey.

Moving now to the freight scene in the 1930s — whilst there were many workings during the day in the Derby area, it was the night hours between 10pm and 6am that saw the most activity, both up and down lines being used to

capacity with fitted freight, class A and class B trains with some mineral trains inserted between the late passenger, mail, parcels and fish trains.

One typical working from Chaddesden left for Derby Junction in time to be joined there to vehicles forming part of the 10pm Rowsley to Derby freight which then made up the 10.40pm departure for Gloucester.

The return working of an early morning Leicester to Rowsley freight train leaving about 2am was booked to make several calls before running main line from Breadsall Crossing to travel through Chaddesden ahead of the 7.25am passenger from Derby to Nottingham, since it would have been delayed by this train which was an 'all stations' to Nottingham. There was no way incidentally to divert a train off the through passenger lines at Chaddesden on to the goods lines there.

In the early 1930s the 2.10am Nottingham to Rowsley freight was an interesting working in that the train engine was then booked to work the first passenger train from Bakewell, running light engine from Rowsley to Bakewell for that purpose.

Other northbound traffic included the 10am from Chaddesden to Normanton which had to run to strict time since it followed the 10.03 Derby-York express from North Junction whilst running ahead of the 10.20 Derby-Manchester passenger train.

Above:
LMSR compound 4-4-0 No 1111 of Longsight shed, Manchester stands at the head of an express from the north at No 6 platform at Derby Midland station on 30 May 1935. *H. C. Casserley*

Below:
The south end of Derby Midland station as it appeared on 28 November 1935 with the original Stephenson train shed still then intact.
LMSR Official, Author's Collection

The 2.10pm 'beer' train from Burton-on-Trent to Leeds was one of only a few booked main line through the passenger platforms, and it is said that station staff would raise their hats in salute as it passed through!

Above:
London, Tilbury & Southend section close-coupled four-coach set with 4-4-2 No 2118 at Borrowash on 29 July 1923.
LMSR Official, Author's Collection

Left:
Local removals service — an LMS container lorry stands outside B. E. Webbe's Hulland Street store on 4 March 1932. Webbe's were contractors for removals undertaken by the LMS.
LMSR Official, Author's Collection

Below left:
Derby station pilot — an old Kirtley 0-4-4WT locomotive — stands awaiting duties beneath the works footbridge. No 1201 was built by Beyer Peacock & Co of Manchester in June 1869 and was broken up in August 1934.
The late W. L. Good courtesy V. Forster

Two important afternoon freight workings were the 4.35pm fully-fitted train from Birmingham to Carlisle which was booked into St Mary's to attach more vehicles worked through on a train from Nottingham and known locally as the 'Tobacco' on account of the consignments of 'Players' cigarettes, etc on board. The other was the part-fitted 4.40pm from Birmingham to Leeds, known locally as the 'Jubilee', whose guard would alight and work the 7.40pm Chaddesden-Birmingham back home again.

In summer months fruit traffic specials passed through Derby both from the Eastern Counties and the Evesham district bound for

Above:
Breadsall Crossing, just north of Derby, a favourite haunt for railway enthusiasts. This view shows ex-Midland 0-6-0 No 3368 hauling a coal train over the crossing on 22 June 1941.
H. C. Casserley

Lancashire, Yorkshire and the North, the empty vans returning the following day.

Quite apart from the above, there was much local trip working from both Chaddesden and St Mary's with return traffic mainly to Chaddesden and included trips for:

i)   the Ripley branch, a working which also conveyed a parcels van picked up from Derby station.

ii) Duffield and Belper, a return afternoon/evening trip working which had to run back to Chaddesden South End to deliver traffic for the 8.50pm freight working from Derby to London.

iii) the Wirksworth branch, the outward working conveying empties for loading at the stone quarries. It was not unknown, when empties were in short supply, to re-direct a train from the Birmingham direction to Wirksworth instead of its proper destination!

iv) Shirland Colliery — a trip which had to be worked by a Class 2F 0-6-0 Freight engine due to the narrowness of the tunnel on the branch. Other trip working in this area included one from the Hasland to service Wingfield Manor Colliery and Stretton (for Ashover) Station Sidings. Johnson Class 3 0-6-0s were later used for this trip.

v)   the Worthington branch, Chellaston and New Lount Colliery.

vi) Sheet Stores (near Trent), where the MR's wagon sheet manufacturing and repair facility was still in intense use at that time, including calls at Draycott and Borrowash.

vii) Spondon power station and the works of British Celanese, synthetic textile manufacturers.

viii) the Locomotive and the Carriage & Wagon Works at Derby with regular supplies of raw materials such as wood, steel and consumables going in and new and repaired locomotives and rolling stock and also spare parts, etc, coming out.

Locomotives for the various trains and for working the yards at St Mary's and Chaddesden and the two Works were, of course, supplied by 4 Shed and worked 'light engine' or in a group to where required.

The LNWR goods station at the west of Derby station, formerly called by that company 'Derby Station Goods' was re-named 'St Andrew's' from 2 June 1924 as a consequence of the grouping and to avoid confusion, the yard being adjacent to St Andrew's Church. Goods traffic dealt with here comprised in the main that deriving from the former NSR and L&NWR lines and destined for the Derby area.

Above:
LMS 'Jubilee' class 4-6-0 No 5627 *Sierra Leone* stands at No 6 platform at Derby Midland with an express for Bristol about 1939.
LMSR Official, Author's Collection

With the possibility of war looming, timetables were prepared in July 1939 for that eventuality and on Monday, 11 September 1939 they were introduced. Initially, all dining and sleeping cars were withdrawn although they were re-introduced after a period and some of the now much slower paced trains, initially limited to 45mph between stops, were accelerated on both main line and secondary services out of Derby, as nationwide.

On the GN passenger services were withdrawn between Derby and Burton and Stafford from 4 December 1939 involving the closure of Egginton Junction, Etwall and Mickleover stations (except for passenger excursion traffic) and the disappearance of the remaining eight daily trains.

For the duration of World War 2 all of the named trains passing through Derby Midland lost their titles, whilst some main line services as well as those on some branches were drastically reduced. In the winter timetable for 1941 however, there was still a good service to London with eight direct trains, three involving a change at Trent and four more via Nottingham where a change was also required.

Services to Manchester were completely recast and journey times lengthened considerably, the overall time to London St Pancras for instance being increased to between 5¼ to 5¾hr.

However, on the Wirksworth branch for instance, the prewar service of six trains each way with two extra on Saturdays was cut to only two each way, the Saturday trains remaining, but all were at different times. The passenger service between Derby and Ripley had been discontinued from 1 June 1930 involving closure of the intermediate stations at Little Eaton, Coxbench, Kilburn and Denby as well as Ripley to passengers, although parcels traffic continued to be dealt with except at Kilburn. The local Trent Motor Traction Co, which ran a frequent service through all the places served and in that year absorbed a number of smaller operators, was advertised as the alternative and was the major factor in the closure of that line.

The Derby to Melbourne and Ashby-de-la-Zouch service and the Derby to Castle Donington and Trent service had suffered a similar fate, being closed on and from 22 September 1930 also in favour of Trent bus services, although again, parcels traffic and goods services continued for thirty years or so and until the Beeching era many excursions trains called at Weston, Castle Donnington and Chellaston.

However, in October 1942 the 8th Railway Company of the Royal Engineers moved from

Northern Ireland to train on the greater part of the Melbourne and Ashby-de-la-Zouch branch which became known as the Melbourne Military Railway, the company being housed at Weston Camp. Prior to this, the section from Chellaston East Junction and Quarry to Smisby had been occupied from 19 November 1939 as a second training centre to Longmoor, using the Derby School of Transport of the LMS for operational classes (see Chapter 5).

The railway was used for exercises in railway construction and bridging, six LNER 'J69' 0-6-0 tanks and eight LMS corridor saloons being the stock and in 1941 six ex-MR Class 1F 0-6-0Ts were hired from the LMS and fitted with air brake equipment. One of these was used to work the regular weekend train services from Quarry into Derby, worked initially by Royal Engineer crews, on Fridays at 18.00hrs with an extra Saturday train at 14.00hr. The railway was handed back to the LMS on 1 January 1945.

Derby itself was fortunate in escaping lightly from bombing raids by the Luftwaffe, but on 15 January 1941, high explosive bombs fell on Derby station, destroying 300ft of the roof, a footbridge, a luggage subway and a 70ft length of Platform 6, killing four passengers and two railway staff and injuring three passengers and five railway staff. Within six days 50% of services were resumed and the station was almost back to normal within a fortnight.

Freight workings through Derby increased during the war, but with heavier loads and slower speeds and as many trains as possible sorted out in the local marshalling yards and started on their journeys during daylight hours to avoid the effects of the blackout.

Extra coal traffic passed through the Derby area, much routed over the Erewash Valley line and via Trent either to London or to Birmingham via the line to Stenson Junction, much coming from the Northumberland and Durham coalfields and being routed by rail instead of via the unsafe east coast sea route as in peacetime, travelling as far as Devon and Cornwall.

There was also a large quantity of traffic related specifically to the war effort, including increased quantities of iron ore from the South and East Midlands on its way to blast furnaces in the North East and Scotland and also a considerable amount of raw materials and merchandise including timber, cement and wool, quite apart from large quantities of munitions. There were, of course, special loads such as the 160ton stator which passed through the Derby area in May 1941 on its way from Newcastle to Coleshill via Derby Friargate and Egginton Junction — a journey which was undertaken on an LNER transformer set with cross rails enabling the load to be moved laterally by up to a foot and which took five weeks of Sunday travel to accomplish!

At the end of the war normality of a kind returned to the Derby railway scene, but many services taken off as a wartime expedient, were never to re-appear.

With the October 1946 timetable three identifiable workings of the former 'Peak Express' and the 'Palatine' were re-established, these being the 10.15am and 4.15pm from St Pancras and the 4pm from Manchester Central. The 'Devonian' working was restored, with a time of 8¾hr from Bradford to Torquay and 3min under 9hr in the reverse direction. The name itself was later still to be restored for the train with restaurant facilities running each way during the summer between Bradford Forster Square and Kingswear, leaving Derby at 12.26pm going south and 3.56pm going north, overall journey times in 1950 being even more extended at 10hr 7min and 10hr 9min respectively. An additional train ran on Saturdays from Teignmouth at 10.15am calling at Derby at 5.05pm going on to Bradford Forster Square for 8.12pm.

After an independent existence of only 25 years, the LMS was about to lose its identity to become part of the nationalised undertaking called 'British Railways', this compared to the MR's 78½ years, more than three times as long — an interesting point.

Below:
Bomb damage at No 6 platform at Derby Midland station after one of the very few air raids in the area on 15 January 1941.
LMSR Official, Author's Collection

Developments under British Railways (1949-1960)

After the formation of British Railways on 1 January 1948 the two Works at Derby slowly became involved in the new standard products of both locomotives and rolling stock. The Locomotive Works continued building 2-6-4T locomotives up to January 1955 although the last 15 were of Riddles new standard design, Nos 80000-9 and 80054-8 and continued turning out the ubiquitous 0-6-0 diesel shunting locomotive as noted previously.

In April 1951 Riddles new Class 5 4-6-0 mixed traffic locomotive No 73000 emerged from the Shops, the first of an eventual 125 of this type built there between then and the emergence of No 73154.

In mid-January 1952, the Fell diesel-mechanical 4-8-4 locomotive No 10100 had

Above:
Ex-LMS compound 4-4-0 No 41064 passing London Road Junction signalbox with an express for the west on 11 June 1949. *H. C. Casserley*

Below:
Riddles BR Standard Class 4 2-6-4T No 80000 completed at Derby in September 1952.
BR Official, Author's Collection

emerged from the Works, a joint development by BR and Fell Developments Ltd, and on 9 March began working the 10.48am from Derby to St Pancras returning at 4.15pm and from the 13th its run was extended to work all the way to Manchester Central rather than it being taken off at Derby. It had a chequered career, acquitting itself reasonably well in service after some modifications, but had eventually to be withdrawn on 21 June 1958 after it caught fire at Manchester Central station. However, BR had already put in hand a massive modernisation plan which included the building of large numbers of diesel locomotives of a variety of types from a number of manufacturers. Designed in the Drawing Office of the CME (LMR) at Derby, two types, the Type 2 1,160hp Bo-Bo and the Type 4 2,300hp 1Co-Co1 diesel electrics were designed concurrently but first to emerge from the Locomotive Works at Derby on 24 July 1958 was the Type 2 No D5000.

It was not until almost a year later that the first Type 4, numbered D1 and to be named *Scafell Pike*, emerged from the same shops on 5 July 1959 and, after naming at Carlisle on 14th, made its first run from Derby to Manchester (Central) on 26 August 1959. Planned for use on fast passenger and parcels services, the class of 10 was later transferred in March 1962 en-bloc to Toton for heavy freight duties where they remained for the rest of their working lives. Two are preserved and No D4 *Great Gable* can be seen in action at the Midland Railway Centre near Ripley, Derbyshire. Nos D1-D10 (later denoted Class 44) were completed at Derby between July, 1959 and February 1960 and were followed by a more powerful 2,500hp version of the class, Nos D11 onwards of which 94 were to be built at Derby between 1960 and 1963, Nos D11-49 (later Class 45) having Crompton-Parkinson electrical equipment and Nos D138-193 (later Class 46) having Brush equipment.

Above:
The first of Riddles Class 5 4-6-0s No 73000 completed at Derby in April 1951.
BR Official, Author's Collection

Above:
Naming ceremony of 'Baby Scot' or 'Patriot' class 4-6-0 No 45509 *The Derbyshire Yeomanry* at platform No 1, Derby station in 1951.
BR Official, Author's Collection

Below:
The Fell diesel-mechanical locomotive No 10100, completed at Derby Locomotive Works in January 1952 and seen here on trial. *P. Baker*

Above:
A BR/Sulzer Type 4 1Co-Co1 diesel-electric locomotive under construction in No 8 erecting shop at Derby in 1960.
BR Official, Author's Collection

The Type 2 diesel locomotive was also subsequently uprated to 1,250hp and after the initial batches of the 1,160hp type, Nos D5000-D5150, emerged from the Works in the period July 1958 to April 1961 the first locomotive of the 1,250hp variety, D5151, appeared from Crewe, Derby following on with Nos D5186-5222, D5233-5299, D7500-7577, D7598-7623 and D7660-7677 between 1963 and 1967.

On 14 June 1957 the final Derby built steam engine, Standard Class 5 4-6-0 No 73154, went into traffic, the last of 2,941 new steam locomotives built in the Works in the period from September 1851.

The Carriage & Wagon Works turned to all steel carriage production in 1948 using

experience gained with the 1939 Liverpool-Southport electric stock and in 1951 the first BR Mk 1 type vehicles appeared, having a gauge profile able to pass over all principal lines without restriction, the works at Derby building 180 corridor seconds and 95 corridor second brakes.

In April 1954, the first light-weight diesel railcars, in a two-car set, appeared from the Carriage & Wagon Works and on 24th went on a first run in the West Riding. Powered by two 125hp Leyland 'bus engines mounted horizontally and with a body made from extruded aluminium alloy sections, the set carried 16 1st and 114 3rd class passengers, BR having re-designated 3rd class as 2nd from 3 June, 1956. Then in October 1956 the first three-car all steel bodied diesel railcar set emerged from the Carriage Works, this time with the 150hp BUT below floor engines on the single power car. By January 1958 the Works had produced

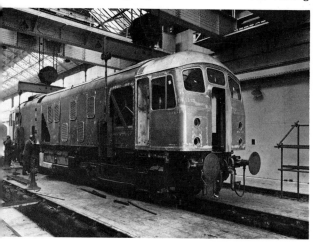

Left:
A BR/Sulzer Type 2 Bo-Bo diesel-electric locomotive being 'bogied' in the diesel new work bay of No 8 erecting shop at Derby in 1958.
BR Official, Author's Collection

500 railcars and by October 1959 the 1,000th — such was the rate of production. By the end of 1955 the 1,000th all steel Mk 1 coach, No M24900, had also been completed.

Staff training

The Locomotive Works had already done pathfinder work with the establishment of an apprentice training school in 1947 following E. J. Larkin's report of March 1943, and approval for the erection of the first school at Derby by the LMS in April 1946. Opened after Easter, 1947 at a cost of £49,000 and with a first intake of 30 apprentices, the school was officially opened by Sir Robert Burrows, Chairman of the LMS on 4 December, 1947. Under Chief Instructor Harold J. Thomas, the school went from strength to strength and as elsewhere, a further school of limited scope was opened in the Carriage & Wagon Works on 2 April 1951 under Chief Instructor Albert Ward. Full facilities were available by 19 March 1957, when Sir John Benstead, CBE, formerly BTC Deputy Chairman, performed the formal opening ceremony.

Subsequent specialist career management training was already being catered for at the School of Transport which the LMS set up at the instigation of Sir Josiah Stamp as the first railway staff training college in Great Britain.

The building was designed in the 'British Georgian tradition' by William H. Hamlyn, FRIBA, the principal architect of the LMS, and constructed by Holliday and Greenwood who completed the work in only 10 months.

Above:
A BR lightweight diesel railcar unit on a trial run near Derby in 1954.
BR Official, Author's Collection

Below:
The diesel railcar engine repair shop in Derby Locomotive Works.
BR Official, Author's Collection

Accommodation comprised a Hall of Transport 118ft long×47ft wide with two murals by Norman Wilkinson depicting travel by land and sea, plus class rooms, a lecture hall, five

Above:
**Apprentices hard at work in the Carriage &
Wagon Works training school.**
BR Official, Author's Collection

Below:
**Derby station reconstruction and Fowler 2-6-4T
No 42336 with a works train in No 1 Platform on
16 September 1954.** *P. H. Wells*

A variety of courses, relating mainly to
railway operating practice, using a fully
operational scale model section of track, and
various aspects of motive power, was initiated
under the control of the school's first Principal, Brigadier L. Manton.

As previously mentioned, it became the No 2
Railway Training College of the Royal Engineers during World War 2, and from 1946 to
1951 its work was mainly concerned with the
postwar rehabilitation of station masters,
controllers, permanent way staff and commercial representatives, and courses were established for locomotive shed masters and also
diesel traction, for which a special diesel
demonstration wing was added in the 1950s.

The first mechanical and electrical engineering courses started in 1956 since which time
the scope of courses has expanded. Further
building extensions were added so that by
1960 up to 85 students could be in residence
attending up to 26 courses a year providing
training for around 700 staff. In 1958 the
operating courses had been replaced by middle
management courses and these continued
until 1976 when the central training school for
the Signal & Telecommunications department
was set up, and the management courses were
transferred to The Grove, Watford, the school
then being re-titled the Railway Engineering
School.

Today, the school caters for about 1,000

class rooms, a dining room and kitchen, a
lounge, a games room and private study
bedrooms for up to 50 residential students on
both ground and first floors. The opening
ceremony, which took place on 23 July 1938,
was performed by Rt Hon Leslie Burgin,
Minister of Transport.

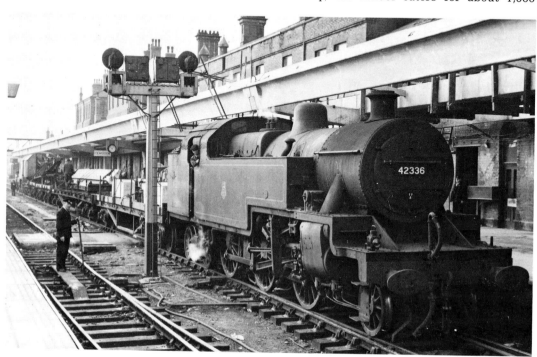

pupils a year attending up to six simultaneous week-day courses of from one to four weeks duration with specialist instructors drawn from their respective BR departments and course contents ranging from basic appreciation to advanced level. Day-to-day control of the school is vested in the Principal assisted by the Chief Instructors and the Bursar, with ultimate control, at the highest level, lying with the Governing Committee chaired by the Board Member for Engineering and Research. Each of the user departments has a Training Advisory Group chaired by a senior officer who is also a member of the governing committee.

Changes at Derby Midland station

In 1952 a £200,000 modernisation plan was put in hand at Derby station which involved the complete demolition of the Stephenson train shed and the erection of individual roofing for each platform supported on reinforced concrete pillars and beams with a new central footbridge of similar construction, the work, largely made necessary by the wartime bomb damage, being completed in July 1954. It must be said that the new scarcely harmonised with

Above:
Ex-LMS compound 4-4-0 No 41157 leaving Derby Midland with a local train for Manchester in July 1959. *T. G. Hepburn/Rail Archive Stephenson*

the original main station buildings of Thompson's design, plus the MR additions, which were tidied up but otherwise remained as they were.

The modernisation process was completed by the end of 1955 with a refurbished refreshment room on Platform 1 providing bar and cafeteria services, kitchen, refrigerated cellar and improved staff amenities, whilst on Platform 4/6 a new refreshment room was provided in a prominent position at the foot of the new overbridge at the south side, replacing an old refreshment room which was demol-

Below:
Fine shot of the north end of Derby Midland station on 24 May 1959 as LMS compound 4-4-0 No 41157 pilots Stanier Class 5 4-6-0 No 44846 on a down Manchester express. *R. C. Riley*

Stanier Class 5 4-6-0 No 45280 approaching Derby Midland station in July 1959 with a relief train from Birmingham.
The late J. A. Fleming courtesy MR Trust

Below:
An evocative scene on No 4 shed at Derby in the mid-1950s with 'Claud Hamilton' 4-4-0 No 62564 on shed after having worked a local train in from Lincoln. *The late J. A. Fleming, courtesy MR Trust*

ished. In addition, two new cigarette and confectionery kiosks were built, one in the booking hall and one on Platform 2/3.

The old MR Superintendent's Office block which had become headquarters for the operating of the Midland Division of the LMS was, however, demolished subsequent to the transfer of work and staff to the new Division at Nottingham and centralisation of LMR operating activities at Crewe, only a curtain wall remaining alongside Platform 1, although this too has recently been demolished as part of the station rebuilding plan. The space was given over to car parking.

Changes to services

Returning to train services the 'Palatine' eventually reappeared in the September 1957 timetable when the name was bestowed upon the existing restaurant car business express leaving St Pancras at 7.55am which reached Derby at 10.21am and Manchester Central at 11.45am, the return working being the 2.25pm from Manchester, arriving at 4.05pm at Derby and 6.20pm at St Pancras.

On 16 September 1957, the pedestrian steam-hauled local service between Derby and

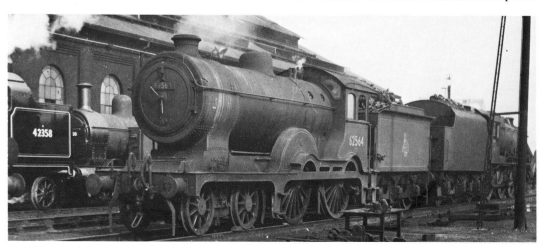

Crewe, over the old NSR route, was changed to diesel railcars. Trips like the one your author made on 29 March 1953 on the footplate of 2-6-0 No 42847 with the 8.25am from Derby with a booked arrival of 10.41 in Crewe and no less than 13 intermediate stops, at an average speed of 22½mph became a thing of the past.

In the 1940s and 1950s Derby-Crewe services were favourite turns for running in both

Below left:
Laying out new permanent way in the Way and Works sidings opposite to the No 4 shed at Derby in 1950. *BR Official, Author's Collection*

Below right:
The new depot at Etches Park, Derby, notably short of standing stock in September 1985. *Author*

Above:
BR Standard Class 2 2-6-2T No 84007 near Pear Tree & Normanton station on 19 July 1957 with the 5.16pm local train from Burton-upon-Trent. *R. J. Buckley*

new and repaired locomotives from Crewe Works, which used to move on to the old NSR shed sidings until wanted for the return working. Locomotive types included Stanier Class 5 4-6-0s (occasionally Scottish Region rarities) 2-6-4Ts, and even rarer a 'Jubilee' class 4-6-0, 45700 *Britannia* appearing on a memorable occasion one evening.

In the 1950s the Derby to Nottingham and Lincoln service was being regularly worked by ex-LNER engines from Lincoln shed including K2 class 2-6-0s, ex-GCR Class A5 4-6-2Ts, ex-GCR 'Director' Class D11 and ex-GER

Class D16 4-4-0s and the occasional ex-GCR Class J11 0-6-0, although underpowered for its task. These services also became a diesel multiple-unit duty from 4 April 1958 and the Lincoln to Derby and Derby to Crewe services were eventually united in a common working timetable from 7 May 1973 subsequently advertised as such but in future running alternatively from Crewe to Lincoln/Grantham due to the Midlands link services from Birmingham to Nottingham.

A new diesel depot was built on Etches Park on the site of former sidings and brought into use in 1959, work being completed the following year.

The old carriage sheds were cleared away to permit a re-modelling of the stabling sidings. The new five road depot split into two main sheds provides maintenance facilities for mainly diesel railcar units in the three road shed and carriages in the two road shed nearest to the London line.

Between the depot and Derby station the carriage sidings provide normal servicing facilities for rolling stock complete with a carriage washing plant installed in recent years, whilst nearer the station the site of the old No 4 shed was laid out with carriage storage sidings, the only remains of No 4 shed being the two buildings, linked by the old end wall, which are used as a signing-on point, and as mess rooms, canteen, etc as mentioned earlier.

By the summer of 1960 Derby Midland had a total of 112 trains either calling at or starting from the station on weekdays, with 68 'Saturdays Only' trains not reflecting weekday services and 10 Friday evening holiday trains for overnight journeys to the West Country holiday resorts, the northeast and Scotland. Through services were provided from Derby to such places as Weston-super-Mare, Bournemouth, Penzance, Kingswear, Sheringham, Gorleston-on-Sea and Yarmouth, Scarborough, Bridlington and Filey Camp, and also to Glasgow (St Enoch) serving in each case the many resorts en route.

On 4 July 1960 a 'De luxe' diesel express 1st class only train, the 'Midland Pullman', was introduced between Manchester Central and London St Pancras with a 7.45am departure from Manchester, arriving in St Pancras at 11am and stopping only at Cheadle Heath, but the train avoided Derby by taking the route through Chaddesden. Essentially a businessman's train the service survived only until 15 April 1966 when the West Coast route out of Euston to Manchester had been electrified.

Local services beyond Matlock on the route through Rowsley to Manchester ceased on 6 March 1967 but the route into Central continued in use until 1 January 1968 when express services were switched to Piccadilly,

Below:
Etches Park carriage sidings, Derby which provides stabling and servicing facilities for rakes of coaching stock and diesel multiple-units, and which occupies part of the site of the old No 4 shed, as it was in September 1985.
Author

running via Chesterfield as from 1 July of that year with the complete closure of the line between Matlock and Peak Forest Junction.

Derby Nottingham Road station had also closed on 6 March 1967. Since the war only a handful of trains had called and by 1957 it had had only four workmen's trains calling each weekday, comprising in the morning the 7.11 ex-Darley Dale and the 7.26 ex-Sheffield and in the evening the 5.14 to Chesterfield and the 5.52 to Darley Dale (both SX) with a single extra train on Saturdays, the 12.22 to Darley Dale, and no service on Sundays.

The GNR line through Derby Friargate had

Above:
Ex-L&NER Class J39 0-6-0 No 64728 heads away from Derby past Spondon signalbox on its way to Nottingham and Lincoln with the 12.20pm working on 19 June 1954. *R. J. Buckley*

Below:
Stanier 'Jubilee' 4-6-0 No 45662 *Kempenfelt* heads past Derby Junction signalbox with a Sunday Bristol-Bradford express on 24 May 1959. *R. C. Riley*

become part of the LNER from 1 January 1923, and from 1 January 1948 it became part of the Eastern Region and although all LNER lines

Above:
An ex-LNER 'B1' class 4-6-0 passes Derby West signalbox on the ex-GNR line with a westbound mixed freight shortly before the line closed. The former engine shed has already been put to industrial use. *P. G. Moore*

Below:
Ex-LNER Class B1 4-6-0 No 61392 stands at Derby Friargate station with a westbound excursion about 1960. *M. Bland*

west of Nottingham were transferred to the London Midland Region from 2 April 1950 operation of the line on a penetrating principle remained in the control of the Eastern Region Central Train Timing Office at Liverpool Street until 1957.

The prewar Saturdays only service from Birmingham New Street to Skegness via Burton and Derby Friargate was restored on 21 June, 1947, usually worked between Burton and Skegness by a Colwick 'K2' or 'K3' class

2-6-0 locomotive and calling at Egginton Junction to connect with the Derby Midland to Crewe service. On 3 July 1954, the Nottingham Victoria to Llandudno service via Friargate was restored after a lapse of 40 years but now as a complete train with further coaches ex-Burton attached at Tutbury. From 5 July 1958 this service was extended to start from Leicester Central and ran for the last time on 2 September 1961. Six months later, on 3 March 1962, Egginton Junction station was closed to all passenger traffic followed by Mickleover station on 3 February 1964, Breadsall having earlier closed to all traffic from 6 April 1953.

A casualty of the Beeching report, the whole line was, however, soon to close for the last passenger train left Derby Friargate at 10.10pm on 5 September 1964 hauled by Ivatt 2-6-0 No 43160 bound for Nottingham Victoria and all passenger traffic officially ceased from 7 September 1964.

Derby Friargate station was closed, and the section between Nottingham and Burton-on-Trent became a freight only line bringing to an end 86 years of passenger working.

On the freight side in June 1950 the GNR line was still handling a large amount of Freight traffic, there being 18 up line trains and 18 down line trains each weekday except Mondays, the majority running between Burton and Colwick, exceptions being milk traffic from Grindley to Derby and returning empties. However, a rapid decline in Freight in the mid-1950s was reflected in traffic using the line. Track on the Duke Street branch was lifted in 1952 except for the section from Derby East to Brown's Siding (Lodge Lane Mill) which

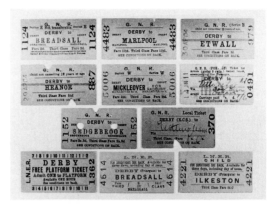

remained open until 1960. Friargate (Goods) eventually closed on 4 September 1967 and Etwall's facility on 6 May 1968 together with the whole section of line from Derby Friargate to Stanton Junction, whilst the Egginton Junction to Derby section was retained for a while after singling for use by the Research & Development Division of the BRB as a test track, the Derby warehouse being used for storage.

However this line was later cut back to Mickleover, releasing the section from there to

Derby Friargate for a major road improvement scheme for the A38 Leeds-Exeter trunk road and the remainder of the land for industrial development purposes.

A farewell tour of the former GN lines in Nottinghamshire and Derbyshire, made by the Stephenson Locomotive Society in a six-car diesel multiple-unit on 4 May 1968, carried the last passengers over the Friargate line and although many reminders still remain including the magnificent Handyside bridge over Friargate, Derby, the bustling activity of this line which once intruded into Midland territory, a commercial venture which hardly paid the GN, is now a mere memory, and my own rememberances of visits to Slack Lane engine shed or the staircase landing, which gave access to the yard from Old Uttoxeter Road, to view a 'B17' 4-6-0 or 'Footballer' as we knew them, shunting below, are tinged with regret that I never thought to capture such scenes on film.

The main goods warehouse at Friargate is still in use for industrial purposes, although the basement is now sealed off, but standing on the former platforms of the Friargate station, where nature has taken a strong hold and trees and bushes abound, it is difficult now to remember how the area looked in its railway heyday.

The motive power scene
The varieties of motive power working through Derby Midland inevitably changed over the years as the older types were scrapped in favour of new locomotives. In Matthew Kirtley's day he had quickly moved from the early small and inadequate locomotives of the

pre-MR companies to his own 2-2-2 and later 2-4-0 designs for passenger work with the 0-6-0 and some 2-4-0 tender locomotives for goods work. With the advent of Johnson the 4-4-0 type was introduced for working express passenger services apart from a brief fling with 4-2-2s in the last decade or so of the 19th century. Johnson's most successful express passenger locomotive in later years was the compound 4-4-0 which continued to be the mainstay of express passenger motive power working alongside the 'Belpaire' boilered 4-4-0s right into LMS days.

The branch line duties round Derby were well covered by Johnson's 0-4-4T and 0-6-0T engines which lasted well into BR days, whilst for freight work the 0-6-0 goods tender engines continued in great numbers as the predominant form of motive power, frequently in multiple of two or even three, despite the production in 1914 of a powerful 2-8-0 design for the Somerset & Dorset line in Fowler's time as CME. Fowler's mixed traffic 2-6-0 design or 'Crabs' as they were nicknamed, appeared in 1926 and were to be seen on both freight and passenger trains. His 2-6-4T appeared in

Below:
Stanier 'Jubilee' class 4-6-0 No 45561
Saskatchewan **heads out of Derby Friargate with a Skegness-Birmingham holiday train on 29 August 1964.** *J Cupit*

Bottom:
Caprotti valve-geared Stanier Class 5 4-6-0 No 44745 enters Derby Midland station with an express for Bristol on 16 September 1954. *P. H. Wells*

December 1927 followed by his 2-6-2T in March 1930 and the former were to be seen on local passenger services.

The above types, many of the older ones now in re-built form, continued to work the bulk of traffic in the Derby area, but by 1928 're-built' 'Claughton' 4-6-0s were to be seen on such workings as the 'Devonian'.

Stanier's arrival in 1932 produced an eventual change in the Derby motive power scene and the appearance of his 'Jubilee' and Class 5 4-6-0s in 1934 began a steady decline in the use of the compounds on the faster expresses, the 'Caprotti' valve-geared Class 5 4-6-0s of 1948 taking over many of the 'Devonian' workings between Bristol and Bradford. Stanier's 2-8-0 freight locomotive of 1935 took over some of the heavy mineral and freight train workings, whilst his version of the 2-6-4T introduced in the same year, found a use on local passenger trains along with Fowler's earlier design.

Above:
Ex-LMS 'Royal Scot' class 4-6-0 No 46152 *The King's Dragoon Guardsman* leaving Derby Midland on 10 July 1958 with the 10.25am from Manchester Central to London St Pancras. *R. J. Buckley*

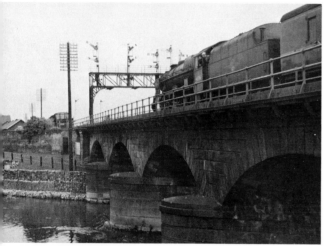

The arrival of Ivatt as CM&EE in February 1946 brought the introduction into the Derby scene of his '1200' class 2-6-2T engines and his '6400' class 2-6-0 tender engines, one of the latter, No 6443, serving as Derby station south end pilot for many years, shunting the dock and attaching and detaching vehicles as required and trip working trains of coaching stock to and from the Etches Park carriage sidings. His other design, the Class 4MT 2-6-0 of the '3000' class, unflatteringly known as 'pigs' by the train-spotters of the day, were to be seen on local services to and from Nottingham from both the Derby Midland and Friargate stations.

In 1960, by which time Riddles range of standard BR steam locomotives were to be seen working alongside MR locomotives up to a century older, services between London (St Pancras) and Manchester (Central) passing through Derby were being worked by 'Jubilee' 4-6-0s and 'Britannia' 4-6-2s whilst a variety of motive power was to be seen on the NE/SW route including Stanier Class 5 and 'Jubilee' 4-6-0s, Fowler 'Royal Scot' and 'Patriot' class 4-6-0s and Riddles Class 5 4-6-0s. Locals to Manchester were normally in the hands of Stanier Class 5 4-6-0s and those to Sheffield and Nottingham by a wide variety of types whilst shorter distance locals to Bakewell and Darley Dale were usually being hauled by a Fairburn 2-6-4T.

Above:
BR Standard 'Britannia' class 4-6-2 No 70021
Morning Star **leaves Derby Midland with an**
express for London St Pancras in September
1958. *The late J. A. Fleming, MR Trust Collection*

Freight traffic was entrusted to the Fowler 'Crab' 2-6-0s or Riddles Class 9F 2-10-0s with occasional interlopers such as an ex-LNER 'B16' 4-6-0 working the Burton-York beer train, whilst local freight trip working was in the hands of Fowler Class 4F 0-6-0s or the even older Johnson Class 3F 0-6-0 and the occasional Kirtley Class 2F 0-6-0. The veteran double-framed 0-6-0 No 58110, built by Dubs in March 1870, a memorable sight for spotters a decade before as she struggled with a trip working from Chaddesden round the curve to Derby Junction, had succumbed to the cutter's torch in 1951.

Above right:
Ex-LNER Class B1 4-6-0 No 61157 leaves
platform 6 of Derby Midland station on 27 June
1959 with a Scarborough to Birmingham
special. *T. G. Hepburn/Rail Archive Stephenson*

Right:
Ex-LMS 'Patriot' class 4-6-0 No 45519 ***Lady***
Godiva **leaves Derby Midland with a northbound**
'Devonian' express on 25 March 1959. *R. C. Riley*

The modern scene and its changes (1961-1985)

With the strong emergence of first diesel and then electric forms of motive power and their rapid ascendancy over steam, much needed to be done by way of training drivers for these new forms of traction and a massive programme was initiated, a consequence of which was the opening of a diesel driver training school at Derby on 5 July 1961 in a new £21,000 prefabricated timber building erected by Vic Hallam (Contractors) Ltd over a period of five months on a site opposite the CME's design offices on the London Road. The opening ceremony was performed by Sir William A. Stanier, former CME of the LMS.

3,700 footplate staff had already been trained in the former Siddals Road training school opened near the station in 1955, but the new school had an expected intake of 1,500 trainees annually of which 40 were on the course of any one time. Railcar drivers spent two weeks in the classroom followed by a week's practical experience driving under supervision.

Under British Railways' largest-ever re-signalling scheme a new power box was built at Derby along with others at Trent and Saltley, controlling in all 242 route miles and replacing 180 old type mechanical signal-boxes. Approval for the scheme was given in September 1965 and the new box at Derby was erected on a site in the angle between the London and Burton lines and adjacent to the lines affording rail access to the Carriage & Wagon Works. Part of the site had formerly been occupied by the Pullman Car shops and part by the former NSR's locomotive depot.

The box replaced 37 conventionally operated mechanical signalboxes in the Derby area and also the 166 signalmen responsible for their operation, and only six of the old boxes were retained as shunting frames.

Below:
Derby power signalbox, now with a pitched roof after the original flat roof gave trouble. *Author*

The new box, built by E. Wood & Son Ltd, and with equipment supplied by the Westinghouse Brake & Signal Co Ltd, was commissioned on 14 July 1969 and then controlled 77¾ route miles and 177¾ track miles, 196 points, 113 controlled signals, 85 automatic or semi-automatic signals and 79 position light ground signals giving 472 signalled routes on 390 indicated track-circuits. Its control area extended from Tamworth and Alrewas in the west to Stretton near Clay Cross in the north and Spondon and Weston-upon-Trent in the east, at which three latter points it linked up with the Trent control area.

The interlocking at Derby covers only the station area and its immediate approaches, all of the passenger through platforms now being capable of bi-directional working. There were nine satellite interlockings at Wichnor Junction, Leicester Junction, Wetmore Sidings, Chellaston, Stenson Junction, Melbourne Junction, Breadsall, Duffield and Ambergate. To minimise delay during temporary faults, the signalman can override the remote control and initiate automatic working on through routes. At Stenson Junction for example, where there are two double-track branches (the lines to Crewe and Trent) in addition to the main lines, routes can be set up for automatic working in any of eight combinations.

The Derby box was originally built with a flat roof but considerable problems were encountered with water permeating through into the box interior so a further contract was let to provide a pitched concrete tile over-roof to cure the problem as on other similar boxes elsewhere.

Derby works progress
Returning to Works matters — on 20 September 1963 the last planned steam locomotive repair was completed and BR Standard Class 4 4-6-0 No 75042 left the erecting shop in steam. After a short ceremony and speeches by the

Above:
The busy interior of Derby power signalbox on 23 September 1985 showing the extensive train indicator panel and control staff. The Derby Midland station train announcer is seated on the right. *Author*

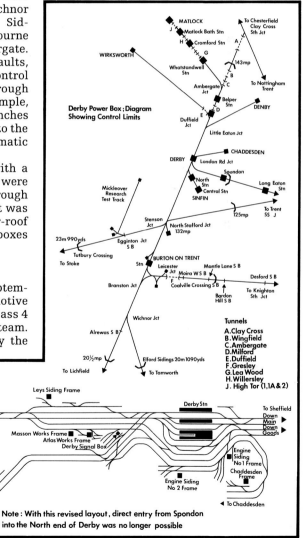

Above:

The last steam locomotive to be officially repaired at Derby Locomotive Works leaves the erecting shop on 20 September 1963 in the shape of Riddles BR Standard Class 4 4-6-0 No 75042.
BR Official, Author's Collection

Below:

The annual Horticultural Society Show and Works Open Day has long been a magnet for both gardeners and railway enthusiasts alike as this view clearly shows. Exhibits on this occasion include 4-6-2 No 46256 *Sir William A. Stanier FRS*, 4-6-2 No 70048 *The Territorial Army 1908-1958*, 0-6-0 diesel shunter No D2394 and on the extreme right the preserved Midland Railway Compound 4-4-0 No 1000. *BR Official, Author's Collection*

Works Manager T. F. B. (Freddie) Simpson and the then Lady Mayor of Derby, Councillor Mrs E. J. Mack, the assembled workforce cheered as the locomotive cautiously edged her way down the Works sidings. Since that date LNER Pacific No 4472 *Flying Scotsman* has received attention in the Works and 'Jubilee' class 4-6-0 No 5690 *Leander* and ex-LMS 0-6-0T No 16440 have received major repairs there.

Less than four years later it was the turn of the Works to bid farewell on 29 April 1967 to the last new diesel locomotive, No D7677, to be built up to the present time, the 1,000th diesel, No D7667, having been completed earlier that year on 28 January.

There was to be no more new locomotive

building until June 1977 when the first of six APT power cars, Nos 49001-6, appeared with due ceremony. One of these — 49003 — was named *City of Derby* at a ceremony in the Litchurch Lane Works (as the Carriage & Wagon Works had by then been renamed) on 7 June 1978. The nameplates have been transferred to IC125 power car No 43107 at a ceremony at Derby station on 7 May 1986 performed by the then Mayor of Derby, Councillor Harry Mathews.

In the early 1960s the resurgence of containerisation as a means of moving bulk traffic on rail, road and by sea, which had seen popularity in LMS days, saw the Litchurch Lane Works in the forefront of BR manufacture of lightweight containers for 20, 30 and 40ft in length not only for BR Freightliner services, but also for private industry and various shipping agencies. A special shop was turned over to containers and flow line production was inaugurated.

The Litchurch Lane Works was also venturing into other new areas of work and 1962 saw the construction of 169 vehicles for the London Underground Central Line, the first of this type to be built in BR Workshops, whilst during 1964-65 an order for 50 four-car AM10 25kV ac electric multiple-units for use on the London Midland's electrified lines in the London and Birmingham areas, was completed.

In 1963 the workshops of British Railways

Above:
An 'AM10' suburban unit, built in the Derby Carriage and Wagon Works in 1964 on the No 4 traverser used to move vehicles sideways between roads in the shop and between shops.
BR Official, Author's Collection

Below:
A large stock of Bell containers, just some of the vast range of such containers built in the Derby Carriage and Wagon Works during the boom in this type of transportation in the early 1960s.
BR Official, Author's Collection

were separated from its other functions to become British Railways Workshops with headquarters temporarily located at Castlefields House in Derby town centre pending completion of the second phase of what is now the Railway Technical Centre. The Division was subsequently reformed in 1970 to become British Rail Engineering Ltd with authority to compete for non-BR contracts both in Britain and for the export market.

Derby was chosen as an ideal centre for the location of the workshops headquarters, lying within the triangle York, Crewe and Rugby, and already having two main workshops and several other important railway establishments including the Research Department. The BREL headquarters was subsequently moved

to the new Derwent House at the Railway Technical Centre (as the extended site there, which included the new Engineering Research Laboratories, became known), the new building being opened by Rt Hon Mrs Barbara Castle, then Minister of Transport, on 22 June 1972.

1964 saw trials of the XP64 prototype train of modified Mk 1 vehicles built for evaluation and early in 1964 the first of an eventual 321 Mk 2 type vehicles emerged from the Carriage & Wagon Works of which an eventual total of 1,892 of the Mark was to be turned out as follows:

Year introduced	Type	Quantity built	Comments
1964	Mk 2	321	Vacuum braked
1967	Mk 2a	289	Air-braked
1969	Mk 2b	111	Air-braked, corner-doors
1969	Mk 2c	250	Air-braked, corner-doors, provision for air-conditioning
1971	Mk 2d	275	Air-braked, air-conditioned, ac power supplies
1972	Mk 2e	174	Air-braked, air-conditioned, ac power supplies
1973	Mk 2f	471	Air-braked, modified air-conditioning, new type seating
TOTAL —		1,891 + 1 departmental coach	

Other Mk 2 vehicles were also built for the CIE and for the Guinea Bauxite Co.

The natural successor to the Mk 2 was the Mk 3 which first appeared from the Derby Works in 1975, following the building of prototype vehicles Nos M11001 and M12001 (now forming part of the Royal train in a new guise) together with eight others for the prototype Class 252 High Speed Train in 1972.

With an overall length of 23m over gangways, increased seating capacity and designed to run at 125mph, the production version of these vehicles has been turned out from the Derby Works since early 1975.

HST Class 253 trains incorporating Derby built Mk 3 coaching stock were put into service on the Western Region on 4 October, 1976 and the first Class 254 set was handed over to the Eastern Region on 7 September 1977. Derby's first complete scheduled HST services on the NE/SW route commenced officially with the new May timetable of 1982 (with reversion to loco-haulage for some heavily loaded services) but HST's began infiltrating these services from 5 October 1981. They are now in use in HST formations and in locomotive-hauled trains on all but one region of BR and, after heavy utilisation, are currently being refurbished internally in conjunction with external repainting in new InterCity livery.

A loco-hauled restaurant buffet version with

Below:
The Mark 3a carriage body production line in 'U shop at the Derby Carriage and Wagon Works.
BR Official, Author's Collection

a kitchen and seating 17 in 1st class style seats appeared in 1979 and other catering variants (TRSB, TRUK and TRUB types) were built for inclusion in High Speed Train sets.

Following the catering vehicle designs came the Mk 3 Sleeping Cars in 12 and 13 compartment versions, also designed in the DM&EE drawing offices at the Railway Technical Centre as were the earlier versions.

Numbered in the range 10500-10646, they were the next new vehicles to appear from the Carriage & Wagon Works, making their public debut on services between King's Cross and Aberdeen in January 1983.

The most recent new vehicles have been the

38 First Open Mk 3b coaches, similar to Mk 3a's but with modified interiors and IC80 (APT) style 1st class seating which began to emerge from the Works in April 1985. Designed for use on the Liverpool and Manchester Pullman services to Euston they were introduced with the May 1985 timetable, replacing the older vehicles of the Manchester Pullman set also turned out by the Works in the mid-1960s. Three further Mk 3b vehicles, this time brake first opens, were due to be completed by the end of 1985.

Following the construction of two pre-production prototype bodyshells in the Works in 1974-5, the modern bay of the lifting shop (U) was laid out and equipped for the production of the 38 trailer cars for the APT-P prototype trains.

With bodyshells constructed of 23 full length, wide aluminium extruded sections welded at their edges, the vehicles were made up in rakes of six trailer cars in the Works and subsequently two rakes were united with two centrally placed cabless power cars Nos 49001-6, which were built between June 1977 and December 1979 and delivered from the Locomotive Works as mentioned previously, to make up a 6+2+6 standard formation.

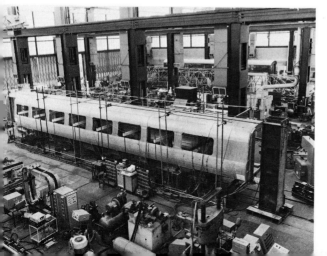

Trials of the first power car took place on 25 July 1977 the first trailer rake being tested on 7 July 1978 and the first APT train main line run occurred on 26 April 1979.

Research matters

The story of railway research at Derby is a fascinating one going right back to trials with smoke consumption apparatus and brick arches in MCR days.

The MR first established a separate engineering testing department in the Locomotive Works during Johnson's regime as Locomotive Superintendent, with other Laboratories in Calvert Street and in 1910 a Textile Research Station was set up at Derby to control and monitor the use and quality of upholstery and other fabrics.

After grouping in 1923, the various research facilities scattered around the LMS system were eventually concentrated at Derby, the paint laboratories amalgamating in 1930, all later to become part of the new LMS Scientific Research Department set up in 1933 with new headquarters on the London Road adjacent to the CME's drawing offices.

These new buildings were designed by H. J. Connal, FRIBA of the Chief Engineer's Department and comprised a laboratory block with some 5,600sq ft of floor space and an adjoining engineering test room and workshop block of some 3,500sq ft.

The steel-framed building, with reinforced concrete floors and roofs, was built by Greenwoods (Mansfield) Ltd of Mansfield, Notts, and F. Jackson & Co of Manchester supplied the furniture and laboratory equipment.

Above:
The Midland Railway test office in Derby Locomotive Works is seen here in October 1895.
MR Official, Author's Collection

Below:
The original LMS scientific research laboratories and workshops on the London Road, Derby, with the Locomotive and the Carriage and Wagon drawing offices beyond. *Author*

The facilities were officially opened on Thursday, 10 December 1935 by Lord Rutherford of Nelson accompanied by Sir Josiah Stamp, the official party travelling from St Pancras by special train appropriately hauled by 'Jubilee' class 4-6-0 No 5665, which had been named *Lord Rutherford of Nelson* by the opener's grandson, Master Pat Fowler, at St Pancras before the trip.

A Chief Metallurgist, a Textile Technologist, a Paint Technologist and an Engineering

Research Officer all now had laboratories at Derby with a total staff of around 150 of whom some 60 were scientific graduates.

In 1935 an open circuit (straight through) type 60mph wind-tunnel was installed in the paint shop at Derby Locomotive Works to the designs of Dr F. C. Johansen, first head of the LMS Research Engineering Section. Based on the National Physical Laboratory designs it was built in the Carriage & Wagon Works utilising a second-hand aircraft propellor and a new motor generator set driven from the Work's mains.

Testing work began in 1936, the LMS wishing to assess the effects of aerodynamic forces on its latest designs including Staniers streamlined LMS 'Coronation' class 4-6-2 and the articulated three-car diesel set of 1938 using 1/24th scale models. Other valuable work included the effectiveness of various types of smoke deflector for steam locomotives, designed to carry smoke from the chimney clear of the driver's cab; the design of coach ventilators; the flow of cooling air for diesel locomotives; wind loadings on platform awnings and the effects of wind on hand and signal lamps.

In 1952 the wind tunnel had to be removed from the paint shop and the opportunity was taken to design a new closed-circuit 100mph wind tunnel incorporating the working section of the old tunnel, but with a new fan. Designed jointly by BR and Airscrew Co of Weybridge and built in sections by Jicwood Ltd, the new tunnel was installed in former LMS horse stables in the Carriage & Wagon Works near to the Research Department, and formally opened by Dr Johansen on 19 October 1953.

It continued in use until 1960 when changing work patterns in the Research Department led to a reduction in its use, and was handed over for re-installation at the Derby College of Technology where it continues in use jointly with BR. From the late 1960s BR work has included aerodynamic studies for both the HST and APT trains and passenger coaches etc, all undertaken by the Aerodynamics Section of the Research & Development Division of the Board.

Early in 1964 the former Horse Infirmary at the Carriage & Wagon Works (in the same group of buildings utilised to house the wind tunnel) was renovated to house the Ultrasonic School, formerly at Stratford Works and which had closed the previous year, and also the Welding School.

Ultrasonic testing utilises the pulse-echo method of flaw detection in vehicle axles and other railway components and structures and the technique is used throughout all BR Regions. Operatives attend a three week course involving both theory and practice and are given a certificate of approval whilst a three-day appreciation course is given to supervisory and technical staff including design engineers. The Welding School likewise provides operator and inspector courses of one week's duration designed to ensure good quality defect-free welds executed in the correct manner by a variety of processes to laid down standards. Appreciation courses are also provided for design engineers, civil engineers staff, etc, to stress the requirements for sound design and the proper application of welding to structures of all kinds.

In September 1961 the contract was placed for new £1¼m engineering research laboratories at Derby on the site of the old Midland Way & Works Stores and Sidings and the old Oil Stores on the opposite side of London Road to the LMS building, construction work being expected to take two years.

Officially opened by HRH The Prince Philip, Duke of Edinburgh, on Thursday 14 May, 1964 the new facilities comprised an Engineering Test Hall, 52m×58m wide, linked to an open courtyard block comprising single laboratories on three sides and a five-storey administration building, now called Kelvin House. Designed by the BRB Chief Architect, Dr F. F. C. Curtis, Dr Ing, FRIBA, and built by William Moss & Sons, construction began in September 1961 work being completed in October 1963 two months ahead of schedule.

The engineering test hall houses the Research Division's Main Workshops and

Below:
Inside the Engineering Test Hall at the Railway Technical Centre showing a London Underground vehicle and a railbus under test and in the centre background the 'Maglev' prototype vehicle. *BR Official*

Above:
The Rolling Stock Development Unit machine shop area with the fitting out tracks beyond.
Author

vehicles preparation area, and is divided into three main areas, one bay being used for the testing of structures from small bridge sections to whole vehicle bodies, the central bay being a machine shop and the third bay being devoted to the instrumentation, fitting out and modification of the Division's own fleet of test vehicles and locomotives as well as vehicles of all kinds under test.

An adjacent Track Research & Soil Mechanics Laboratory, housed in a two-storey building, with an adjacent test hall, undertakes specific studies in those fields.

The Research Division is responsible for all mechanical, electrical and civil engineering research carried out by the British Railways Board including track and structures, vehicle dynamics and mathematical studies employing the latest computers, with programmes largely written and/or developed in house to suit specific BR requirements.

The new block brought many disciplines together for the first time, the Electrical Research Division coming to Derby from London with around 100 staff engaged on communication and signalling systems, current collection, motors and generators, now to rub shoulders with staff from the civil and mechanical engineering division, the chemical research division (also from London) and the scientific services division and also, in due course, with their colleagues in the Centralised Design Office, soon to be set up. Thus scientists and engineers working on a wide range of projects were now in close contact with each other, the intention being that the cross fertilisation of ideas and the free exchange of information would stimulate an innovative atmosphere greatly beneficial to the railway as a whole.

Development of the Railway Technical Centre continued, as previously mentioned, with the erection of Derwent House, officially opened on 31 March 1967 built to house the Headquarters of British Rail Engineering Ltd, the Staff and Services Section, a centralised typing bureau and also the Central Purchasing organisation with a staff of 185 under the control of the Supplies Manager. This group moved from old accommodation at Euston and is responsible for supplying the vast range of everyday needs to operate and maintain the BR network, contracting for the supply of both road and rail vehicles, as well as consumables such as fuel and lubricating oils, uniforms, etc, the total value of all purchases then being in the region of £160/£170 million per annum. The Department is also responsible for the sale of the Board's unwanted assets, with the exception of buildings and land, which range from complete locomotives and items of rolling stock to waste paper, realising at that time some £20m in a year.

The adjacent Trent House opened its doors on 13 March 1967 to receive the first influx of design staff from the old Locomotive Drawing Office of the CME on the London Road, to be joined shortly afterwards by their colleagues from the Carriage & Wagon office. This new block was built to provide centralised accommodation for the design staff of the new Director of Design, with an amalgamation of staff coming to Derby from the former regional design offices of the CME's at Swindon, Doncaster, Eastleigh, Crewe, Glasgow, etc, each with histories dating back to the old pre-grouping (1923) companies and their old loyalties, which were frequently apparent!

This new organisation was now to undertake the mechanical and electrical design, development, testing and modification of all types of locomotives and rolling stock including electric and diesel multiple-units and containers. Only small residual groups of staff remained at the former eight centres to deal with day-to-day problems in the Workshops and on the Regions and to feed back data affecting existing and future designs to the Central Design Office.

Also erected at the centre was the Rolling Stock Development Unit's test hall complete with a Machine Shop and an external weighbridge. The unit, formerly at Darlington, was now housed in new accommodation well equipped to manufacture anything required by way of experiment and test together with a capability to construct and evaluate mock-ups and prototypes. In addition the Plastics Development Unit, responsible for developing and advising on the use of the wide variety of new plastic and other advanced materials, was removed from Eastleigh to the centre and has since been responsible for valuable pioneering work in the application of glass reinforced and other plastics not only for integration within the design of locomotives and rolling stock but also in bridge structures and sections, mast supports, station furniture and fascia unit sections, portable buildings, etc.

Subsequently added have been a further three storey office block, Lathkill House named, like Trent and Derwent Houses, after a Derbyshire river and an Engineering Test Hall, initially built for the Advanced Projects Group with facilities for studying the behaviour of vehicles on track, braking systems, vehicle suspension systems, etc, and a six storey block, Brunel House, opened by Sir Henry Johnson, CBE, then Chairman of the BRB, on 27 August 1971 to house the field trials, fracture mechanics, aerodynamics, instrumentation and chemical research sections and the research drawing office.

Construction of the multi-purpose Advanced Projects Vehicles Laboratory, with a floor area of 1,500sq m, commenced in July 1969 and took a year to complete. A central control cabin, situated above the Superintendent's office and store rooms, monitors the activities of the experimental facilities which include a brake dynamometer, extensive resonance and vibration testing equipment and a clean room.

The Research & Development Division has also the use of two test tracks for vehicle testing purposes, the local one being the section of the former GNR line between Mickleover, a western suburb of Derby, and Eggington Junction where a connection is made with the Derby to Crewe line, a total distance of some 5¼ miles of now singled track with run-round loops at each end. At Mickleover a two road train shed 46m long is provided along with a laboratory, a mess room and a control office, etc. The test length contains a variety of track types and facilities exist for the introduction of track irregularities to monitor ride response.

The second test track is a 13-mile section of the former down line of the MR route between Melton Junction and Edwalton, which includes five tunnels and a three-mile length of straight track which, for instance, enabled the APT-E train to attain high speeds during a series of test runs. Partway along the straight is Stanton Tunnel where aerodynamic tests can be carried out. In places the track is sinuous enabling high speed curving capabilities to be monitored. All tests are in radio contact with a control centre at Old Dalby where there are also workshops, conference and mess facilities.

The former LMS research block of buildings, now renamed Hartley House, today houses the Scientific Services group, the former Locomotive and Carriage & Wagon drawing offices, vacated in 1967 forming an additional 'annexe' for the departments use.

A new technical library block was added in the quadrangle of Kelvin House and opened by Dr Sydney Jones, CBE, a member of the BRB, on 22 June 1972 and provides the centre with a valuable source of technical material and information.

Below:
The Advanced Projects Vehicles Laboratory with a Class 507 unit undergoing tests. *BR Official*

The Railway Technical Centre, by then covering a 23 acre site and with modern office and laboratory accommodation for more than 2,000 staff, at that time represented a total investment of well over £9 million. Each year it receives many visitors, particularly from overseas government departments and railway administrations, who come specifically to see research and technical development work being undertaken in the various departments.

Major research and development projects undertaken have now included a high-speed pantograph for electric trains, advanced bogies for freight vehicles, a new concept in traction motors and perhaps the largest project which began as a by-product of fundamental research into the dynamics of railway vehicles and resulted in the conception in 1967 of the Advanced Passenger Train, the gas turbine powered experimental version of which (APT-E), towards the end of a three year test programme in 1975, ran from London (St Pancras) to Leicester, a distance of 99 miles, in 58min on a curving route which normal service trains then took 1hr 24min to cover.

The pre-production prototype APT, this time with more conventional electric power cars, was a natural development which, despite its problems and very limited use in trial passenger service, has enabled detailed studies of a number of unique design features to be carried out including vehicle tilt and hydrokinetic braking, providing valuable and positive evaluations to be made of such features to assist in the formulation of future vehicle designs such as the Mk 4 coach.

Modern freight traffic trends

Returning to traffic matters in the Derby area — the amount of goods traffic and other freight dealt with at St Mary's had been declining annually and in fact was never to recover from the rapid national decline in rail freight after a peak in 1956.

In 1957 an attempt was made to arrest the fall in receipts by switching services to fitted freight trains run at faster speeds with an emphasis on door-to-door service.

Re-organisations in 1958 saw the opening of one of six new Divisional Headquarters for LM Region traffic at Nottingham on 10 July and on 30 November the lines controlled by the Divisional Operating Superintendent at

Below:
A once common sight in towns — the 'mechanical horse' and its trailer, this one being outside the St Mary's goods depot at Derby in 1962. At that time the depot was still in wide use if a declining one. *BR Official*

Nottingham Midland and Victoria (formerly GCR and GNR) came under a single administration, the District Operating Superintendent at Derby taking responsibility for some of the former GNR Section in the Derby area.

In a rationalisation exercise, work was switched from the smaller marshalling yards to the large yards such as Chaddesden. For instance, the sidings at Little Eaton Junction, which had been used to marshall shipping and export coal traffic off the Ripley branch from the Denby (Drury Lowe) and Marehay Collieries for onward transmission northwards to Manchester and Liverpool Docks, were closed and the traffic re-routed into Chaddesden.

At the same time Ambergate Yard ceased to handle coal traffic from Shirland and Wingfield Manor Collieries and also coal and other traffic ex-Westhouses comprising two pick-up freight trains per weekday.

With the decline and closure of collieries in this area only Denby Opencast remained, the washery there continuing to wash coal from the Westhouses area for a further two years.

In the Burton-on-Trent area, similar closures of collieries saw the traffic formerly using Chaddesden move into decline, the residual train-loads being switched via the Stenson Junction-Sheet Stores Junction line to Toton. This line is heavily utilised by MGR trains for Willington Power Station and other traffic for the West Midlands.

Reconstruction work at Derby St Mary's goods depot in 1959, which included berthing for an extra 32 cartage vehicles and enlargement of the sorting dock, resulted at

DERBY AREA FREIGHT TRAFFIC
Trains attaching and detaching traffic at or for Derby as at 7 October 1974 (Weekdays Only)

SX = Saturdays excepted
MO = Mondays Only
MX = Mondays excepted

F = Fitted   NF = Non-fitted

Code	Time	From	To	Type	Notes
8P75	00.05 MX	Brent	Derby	F&NF	
8E38	22.50 SX	Cardiff	Tinsley		Detach Burton & Derby traffic
6V86 Replaced by	19.42 SX	Derby	Exeter		Ceased 3/3/1975
7G10	19.24 SX	Derby	Bescot		via Leicester commenced 3/3/1975
7E01	20.30 SX	Derby	Tinsley		Conveyed Tyne fitted traffic
8D33	20.36 SX	Derby (St Mary's)	Nottingham (for King's Cross)	F	Conveyed traffic from Edge Hill, Brewery and Stoke
8E49	22.25 SX	Derby (St Mary's)	Whitemoor		Traffic for Norwich NCL & Whitemoor (incl. DMU engines)
8P61	01.55 MX	Etruria	Derby (St Mary's)		Iron ore empties
9P19	08.00 MO	Etruria	Derby (St Mary's)		Iron ore empties
7E08	23.15 SX	Gloucester	Tinsley		Detach Derby traffic at St Mary's
6T20	20.35 SX	King's Cross	Churchyard Sidings		Ceased on 6/1/1975
6E75	21.55 SX	St Pancras	Tinsley	F&NF	Derby traffic from St Pancras, Brent and Luton detached at Leicester
7M22	21.25 SX	Severn Tunnel Junction	Nottingham	F&NF	Detach Derby traffic
7M76	23.08 SX	Whitemoor	Nottingham GYW	F&NF	Detach Derby traffic
8K90	21.58 SX	Warrington (Arpley Sidings)	Cockshute Sidings		Derby traffic detached at Nottingham

the end of that year in the sundries traffic, up to then dealt with at Ashbourne, Burton-on-Trent, Matlock, Ripley and Swadlincote, being concentrated at that depot. The depots mentioned continued to cater for some goods traffic until 1 April 1963 at Ripley, and 2 March 1964 at Swadlincote and Burton-on-Trent except for the goods wharves at Dallow Lane (ex-LNWR), Hay, Horninglow, Moor Street and Shobnall which closed from 6 July the same year and Hawkins Lane (GN), which remained in use until 6 June 1966, and Matlock in use as an unstaffed public siding officially until 4 September 1972.

One stable traffic into the Derby area in season, even from early MR days, was fruit and vegetables which came in not only from the market gardening area around Melbourne, but also from Evesham, Kent, and the Continent, etc. Such traffic was still flowing as late as 1963 although the advent of motor lorries and re-distribution depots throughout the country, which began to make inroads in the early part of this century, caused its eventual demise.

During the 1963 season 'freight rated' fruit was still arriving in Derby from Victoria Docks in London, strawberries from Brest (via Plymouth) and also the Tamar Valley (via Barnt Green) in May and June whilst other fruits in season were conveyed by Special Fruit trains as required as passenger rated loads in through vehicles. Other freight rated fruit traffic from the Continent, loaded in Ferry vans, was worked via Dover and Brent, the Derby traffic being conveyed in the 4K01 (FSX)

from Victoria Docks at 8.40pm for Brunswick, detaching at St Mary's Yard.

Fruit and vegetables from the Eastern Counties were conveyed on the 3M04 (SX) parcels from Peterborough East at 9.50pm to Chaddesden Sidings from where it was trip worked to St Mary's. Other traffic included blackberries from the Gloucester district, fruit from Aylesbury, Harpenden and Shefford and tomato traffic from the Channel Islands via Weymouth during late April and early May.

The Cromford & High Peak line closed to traffic on 30 April 1967 and the stone traffic in the area was then concentrated mainly at Wirksworth, the branch, which had closed to passenger traffic in 1947, remaining in use at the present time solely for this purpose although traffic levels are very low. However, the line was specially re-opened from 25-27 May 1985 when the 'Wirksworth Phoenix' passenger charter services were run from Derby over the line calling at Duffield, the start of the branch connection, with local fund-raising schemes, a similar exercise being repeated on 14/15 September.

St Mary's Yard remained essentially a goods depot and exchange point for traffic passing from west to north and vice-versa, even though in gradual decline.

Below:
A view inside the National Carriers warehouse at St Mary's goods yard, Derby, in mid-September 1985 with the racks loaded with Christmas puddings and other such fare for nationwide distribution. *Author*

Above:
Class 08 0-6-0 diesel shunter No 08428 shunts Derby St Mary's yard after arrival of the trip working from Toton in September 1985. *Author*

Northbound traffic, which had originally to be backed into the yard was afforded easier access when a facing connection was added just beyond the old Nottingham Road station, westbound traffic being halted in the up sidings for St Mary's bound vehicles to be detached. With the opening of Derby Power Box the whole area was re-modelled and subsequently St Mary's ceased to be a goods exchange sidings.

The cattle docks at Derby closed completely from 1 January 1965 and the London Road Wharf closed for all goods traffic on 4 January along with Peartree & Normanton.

On 18 April 1966 the BRB initiated its National Freight Train Plan designed to rationalise wagon load traffic and introduce booked services between concentration points, and clearly this was to affect services at Derby in a major way. However, St Andrew's goods yard remained open for a few more years, but eventually closed on 5 July 1971 except as a private siding facility not available for public traffic.

Chaddesden Sidings was also to lose traffic and by 1965 all marshalling work, with the exception of block traffic which was concentrated at Chaddesden South Junction, had been transferred to Toton. The 'New Bank' sidings were closed and the through main line route was cut under the Multiple Aspect Signalling scheme, Chaddesden becoming a dead end.

It had a short new lease of life as a concentration point for crippled wagons and vehicles surplus to BR requirements were stored there in large numbers for disposal along with surplus coaching stock and excursion stock out of season. The Wagon Shops,

retained on a regional repair facility for items such as hot axleboxes, defective brakegear, etc, were eventually closed in 1982.

Final closure came the following year except for the continued use of the old storage sidings for a sand and gravel extraction scheme on the banks of the River Derwent and spent ballast is still currently being delivered there by the DCE Nottingham both as infil and for re-sale.

St Mary's however, still remains open as a small concentration depot for Speedlink traffic some feeding via Toton into the network. Other traffic includes loads of Butterley bricks forwarded by Speedfreight to Avonmouth, Stratford, Dundee, Southampton, Gateshead, Swansea and Law Junction (Scotland) and MoD traffic to Bicester, Giffen, Pridys Hard (Southampton) and Longtown.

National Carriers Ltd set up in 1968, now occupies the sundries shed built in 1939 and now modernised and extended to cater for traffic arriving and departing in Continental Ferry vans by trip working via Toton.

When first built this depot, with 16 sets of lines, had coped with up to 200 wagons for unloading and despatched up to 200 loaded wagons per shift. A nearby stable housed internal horses, not considered fit for use on public roads, which performed shunting operations in and around the shed.

By September 1985 the NCL depot was handling some 17,000 tons of 'Eurodeker' chipboard arriving from Austria in bulk by Continental Ferry wagon, fertiliser from Hol-

Midland design coal merchants offices at the entrance to St Mary's goods yard, Derby. Each merchant trading from the yard would have his own individual office allocated by the Midland where he kept his records of consignments received by rail and sales to customers. *Author*

A Class 47 Co-Co diesel locomotive hauls a train of bulk cement wagons through No 1 platform at Derby Midland heading west in September 1985. *Author*

land for Sierra UK Ltd, and oil additives for United Guarantee Holdings and shipping out bulk quantities of Christmas puddings and mincemeat from Matthew Walkers of Derby and Heanor. The depot was also storing bulk goods such as wallpaper for call-off requirements.

The main office block and a large section of the transit shed were out of use and clearly there is scope for diversified re-utilisation to a degree.

St Mary's today is but a ghost of its former self, the old town shed, the fruit, tobacco and fish warehouses, the grain warehouse, the lost property warehouse, the old bonded warehouse and the boiler house are derelict; the main office block has already been demolished and only two coal merchants, now under notice, still occupy sites in the yard compared to the once thriving and bustling activity in the now derelict range of 13 coal merchants' offices, all still in use a mere three decades ago.

Towards Caesar Street the unusual double-decked stable block is now leased to a pallet manufacturer while the corrugated iron road motor depot is leased for use as a vehicle workshop. These stables and the earlier stables on Fox Street, which once housed nine horses with two loose boxes and are also now derelict, provided accommodation for the numerous railway horses once to be seen hauling carts and drays delivering or collecting loads for St Mary's depot about the town of Derby.

In place of the four steam locomotives and a five-ton steam crane which once busied themselves about the yard each day, a sole Class 08 0-6-0 diesel shunter now serves the yard, and visiting locomotives arrive and depart quickly with their trains.

The old proliferation of private sidings in the Derby area has almost disappeared. Extensions beyond the end of St Mary's yard serving the Corporation's abbatoir and also the Co-operative Wholesale Society warehouse (1903) where railwaymen worked alongside the Society's own staff — the railway providing a checker, a loader and a porter — have now been lifted, as have the private sidings of engineering firms such as the Parker Foundry Co, Aitons, Fletcher's Masson Works, the 'Atlas Foundry', Eastwood Swingler's 'Victoria Foundry', and a variety of other firms such as Wheeldon's Maltings, the Glass Bottle Co, the Derby Boiler Co and Pountain & Co (Wine importers) who had their own maltings in Wood Street with access to St Mary's Yard, as did the Wheeldon's maltings. There was also an Admiralty Stores Siding accessed through the yard.

Bulk freight traffic passing through Derby today consists largely of oil, steel, coal, aggregates and cement in bulk block trains.

The oil traffic passing through Derby from Phillips Imperial Refinery at Port Clarence on Tees-side to the East Midlands terminal at Long Eaton was instituted at the end of 1969 and was in daily operation by February 1970 with block trains of up to 18 tankers carrying a total of some 200,000gal being unloaded and the oil transferred to storage via 18 discharge points in less than two hours. 1¼ million gallons can be stored for re-distribution.

A similar oil terminal is located at Derby in the original Midland London Road Goods and Coal Depot which has now been converted to a fuel distribution point operated by John Hudson (Economac) Ltd. Similar bulk rapid discharge facilities are provided here also, this oil coming from Bromford Bridge.

Other block oil trains operate through Derby

serving the West Midlands depot at Bromsgrove from Port Clarence and from Llandarcy to Gainsborough in Lincolnshire.

Steel products such as slab steel and coiled steel, carried on bogie flats, also regularly pass through Derby en route from the steel manufacturers in the Sheffield area via Tinsley and Barrow Hill to the car manufacturers and other steel users situated in the West Midlands via the railheads set up for such traffic during the Beeching era at Brierley Hill

Above:

Empty 'Merry-go-round' train hauled by a pair of English Electric Class 20 diesel-electric locomotives heads past St Mary's goods yard on its way to the NCB Denby disposal plant to collect another load of coal for power station use in September 1985. The locomotives are Nos 20005 and 20055. *Author*

Below:

Riddles Standard Class 9F 2-10-0 No 92122 heads an eastbound load of empties near Castle Donnington on 16 October 1965. *M. Mitchell*

and Wednesbury. Other steel traffic passes on its way from Tees-side, Goole, Scunthorpe and Lackenby to Bescot, Etruria, Stoke Gifford and South Wales.

Coal traffic mostly avoids Derby passing in block MGR trains via the Sheet Stores-Stenson line to Willington Power Station, but block trains from the NCB Opencast Executive at the Denby Disposal Plant on the Ripley branch still pass, during daylight hours only, to and from Willington Power Station on an MGR basis, being stabled overnight at St Mary's yard, on Roads 13 or 14. Other coal traffic

moves between Barrow Hill and Didcot, passing through Derby on its way, an example of long distance MGR Working.

Aggregates, the sole reason for the continued existence of the Wirksworth line, continue to flow in the form of limestone trains from the Tarmac Roadstone Holdings' Quarries above Wirksworth along the branch and through Derby (St Mary's) to Hayes, Whitemoor and Kings Lynn. A recent contract has secured the short term future of the branch for this purpose. Other aggregate traffic, in the form of block lime trains, flows through the Derby area on its way from ICI's quarries at Tunstead, Peak Forest via Chinley, Dore and Clay Cross to Margam in South Wales and also to Norton Road (Glos).

Bulk cement passes through Derby from a variety of sources on routes from the Chinnor Cement Works to Bolsover and Barrow Hill, which also receives traffic from Bletchington Works, and other cement traffic from Earle's Sidings (Hope) is moved to Handsworth and Greaves Sidings near Harbury.

Other traffic includes cars from Morris Cowley to Bathgate; Freightliner services between Newcastle and Pengam, and between Leeds and both Bescot and Southampton; chemicals from Severn Beach to York and ballast between Cliffe Hill and Doncaster.

Spent ballast is disposed of from a site at the south end of the former Chaddesden Sidings coming from sites on the former Nottingham Division as previously mentioned.

There is also a vast amount of parcels and mail traffic, passing along all the main rail

Above:
Class 58 diesel-electric locomotive No 58014 working the 12.13pm Lawley Street (Birmingham) to Nottingham freightliner service past Barrow-on-Trent (between Stenson Junction and Sheet Stores Junction) on 4 July 1984. *A. O. Wynn*

Below:
An afternoon limestone train from Wirksworth passes slowly down the branch to Duffield, just north of Derby, behind a pair of English Electric Class 20 diesel-electric locomotives Nos 20005 and 20178 on 20 October 1978. The train is passing the remains of Shottle station.
A. R. Kaye

routes in the late evening and early hours of the morning. Trains depart from Derby to London, Leeds and Northampton whilst ser-

vices such as the Bristol-Newcastle, Bristol-Leeds, Peterborough-Crewe, Manchester-London and Glasgow-Nottingham, are all booked to make a stop at Derby where GPO staff from the nearby Midland Road Sorting Office, just a short distance from the station, have prepared the various batches of mail moved to the station on trolleys hauled by electric tractor for loading on the various platforms.

Other mails arrive constantly during the day by passenger train and are dealt with by the Post Office's platform staff who move the mail

Above:
The GPO mail distribution bay at the south end of Derby Midland's No 1 platform. *Author*

Below:
Brush Class 47 diesel-electric locomotive No D1953 passing Derby with a freight train from the North on 8 June 1968. *David Wharton*

between platforms using the connecting passage beneath the platforms and ramps constructed in 1984 to replace the old hydraulically operated luggage lifts in anticipation of increased GPO traffic.

Above:
New Class 150 diesel railcar unit No 150 002 stands at Sinfin Central on 24 September 1985 having worked the 7.10am service from Matlock. *Author*

As from the night of 27-28 September 1985, when the last Travelling Post Office trains worked over the East Coast route using King's Cross, this traffic was transferred to St Pancras to tie in with the increased use of Derby as a major interchange point for Post Office mail. Ideally situated on the railway network and adjacent to the East Midlands Airport at Castle Donington, Derby thus became a focal point for this bulk traffic, the majority of which is handled overnight.

Further advantages were that the Midland line from St Pancras passes through larger population centres than the East Coast route which was shortly to suffer some disruption during electrification work. TPOs did, however, continue to use that route north of York, being diverted to Derby south of that point.

Passenger traffic trends

Peartree & Normanton station had closed its doors to goods traffic of all kinds from 4 January 1965 and the station had closed to passenger traffic on 4 March 1968. However, it re-opened again as Peartree on 4 October 1976 in conjunction with a new service initiated to two new stations on the former line to Chellaston at Sinfin North and Sinfin Central, built to meet an identified requirement of workers travelling to the Rolls-Royce and other factories in the Sinfin area and a second class only DMU service was initiated. Sinfin North is unique in that there is no public access to the station, only direct access to the Works there. The branch has no service on Saturdays or Sundays and weekday services only operate in the early morning and late afternoon as extensions of the service from and to Matlock respectively. Unfortunately this reopening has never really been a success, only a handful of passengers using the services.

At the same time, the remains of the former MR's main line to Manchester, now reduced to branch line status from Ambergate to Matlock, was converted to single line controlled by electric token in a scheme financed by Derbyshire County Council whose headquarters lie at the end of the line. The branch brings commuters daily from the extremes of the line and intermediate stations to work in the Derby area, the service extending to Sinfin Central in the early morning and late afternoon. November 1984 saw the introduction of

Above:
English Electric 1Co-Co1 diesel-electric locomotive No D221 *Ivernia* entering Derby Midland from the north after having passed through Chaddesden with the 1.55pm London St Pancras to Manchester Piccadilly on 20 July 1962. This particular train, which conveyed restaurant and buffet facilities, ran via Stoke-on-Trent and Macclesfield. *P. J. Lynch*

Below:
Brush A1A-A1A Class 31 diesel-electric locomotive No 31254 arriving at Derby Midland with the 08.12am Leeds-Weymouth on 11 July 1978. *C. J. Tuffs*

the Class 150 diesel multipe-units operating the service under the local name of the 'Sprinter Link', officially launched on the 19th of that month, the class being known under the marketing title of 'Sprinters'.

From 1 May 1972 on Sundays only, the famous 'Thames-Clyde Express' which usually ran via the Erewash Valley line was re-routed to pass through Derby, departing at 12.49 on its way from St Pancras via Nottingham to Glasgow Central, but the arrangement only lasted for the duration of that timetable. It had not done this since alterations made during World War 2 had extended its daily north-

Above:
**BR/Sulzer Class 45/0 1Co-Co1 diesel-electric
locomotive No 45049 *The Staffordshire Regiment
(The Prince of Wales's)* leaving No 4 platform at
Derby Midland on 2 April 1977 with a Leeds-
Penzance express.** *Norman E. Preedy*

bound run to 444 miles for the period of the
national emergency, the train resuming its old
route under its old name from October 1946.

On 6 October 1975 services on the Midland
main line were considerably revised officially
to 'match the present pattern of travel' which
involved the withdrawal or curtailment of
certain trains serving intermediate stations
between St Pancras and Derby and Nottingham connecting with express trains at Leicester, which now became an interchange point, a
service being introduced between Derby and
Leicester to make connection with trains to
and from London, this subsequently being
worked by diesel railcar units.

The 08.01 direct service linking Manchester
with Derby and going on to St Pancras became
a mere Derby to Leicester linking service and
only one up and one down train remained on

the route, these being the 18.06 from Piccadilly
calling at Derby at 19.46 and arriving in
St Pancras at 23.30 (23.13 on Saturdays) and
the 06.52 from London, arriving in Derby at
09.22 and Manchester at 10.54.

The final sleeping car service from Derby,
the 00.26 to Glasgow Central via Sheffield,
Leeds and Carlisle and arriving at 07.47,
disappeared with the introduction of the new
timetable on 3 May 1976.

Recent changes to Derby passenger train
services have included the re-routeing of the
07.15 Master Cutler weekday service from
Sheffield which formerly ran via the Erewash
Valley line but which now leaves Derby at
07.54 and is timed to reach St Pancras at 09.36,
having called at Leicester instead of Kettering
as formerly. The afternoon return service calls
at Derby at 18.12 for Sheffield, whilst the
'South Yorkshire Executive' service operates in
the reverse direction, calling at Derby going
north at 09.33 and at 15.40 on the return leg to
London.

On summer Saturdays there was at the time
of writing (1985) a number of named holiday
expresses as follows:

Name	Destination	Times from Derby
'Cornish Holidaymaker'	Penzance	07.17, 11.10, 12.38
'Torbay Holidaymaker'	Paignton	08.29, 09.34, 10.49
'Dorset Holidaymaker'	Poole	08.49, 09.13, 11.49
'South Wales Holidaymaker'	Cardiff	10.20
'Pembroke Coast Holidaymaker'	Tenby	14.48

Above:
View of Derby Midland station area from the top of Brunel House. The Railway Technical Centre sidings are in the foreground, the weighbridge, carriage sidings and the Locomotive Works are to the right and the station is in the centre distance with St Andrew's goods warehouse to the left. *Author*

There is also an early morning and late afternoon through train to Brighton.

Recent events

In 1983 and as part of a government policy to encourage an arms-length relationship between the British Railways Board and its wholly-owned manufacturing subsidiary, British Rail Engineering Ltd, the headquarters of the latter organisation moved from Derwent House to new premises at St Peter's House, in Gower Street in the centre of Derby. Later in mid-1984 those members of the DM&EE organisation employed on the development of BREL projects relating to both new design work for BR and for foreign customers, were transferred to BREL, forming the basis of a developing Engineering Design organisation. This effectively halved the BRB's design staff, those remaining gradually adopting a conceptual and procurement role rather than one of predominantly manufacturing design as previously.

With the added capability of its own design staff, BREL now actively seeks wider world markets for its products. Already orders have been fulfilled for the Guinea Bauxite Co, Tanzanian Railways, Kenya Railways and Coras Iompair Eireann (Ireland) for passenger coaches based on BR designs. In 1985 further orders were being carried out for CIE and freight vehicles were being built for Ghana Railways.

Now however new products continue to be developed specifically for export markets.

Litchurch Lane's future in main line coach building is firmly wedded to the 'International' coach launched in July 1984. Designed to meet the dimensional, technical and passenger requirements of railway administrations at home and overseas, by the end of 1985 initial orders were already in progress for the Trans-Gabon Railway and the Congo-Ocean Railway in West Africa. A 10-coach demonstration train of International coaches built to the British loading gauge was also being produced for assessment by British Rail.

In response to the international need for lightweight economical passenger vehicles for use on rural and suburban routes BREL joined forces with Leyland Vehicles to build a family of four-wheeled Railbuses using Leyland National bus bodies. For these vehicles a 'Try before buy' policy was introduced and three demonstrator vehicles toured America, Northern Europe and South East Asia respectively on sales promotion tours whilst, following the Class 140 prototype, Class 141 and 142 twin-car series production units were delivered to British Rail.

Building on past experience with the APT vehicles, Litchurch Lane was also responsible for building a four-car prototype tube train for London Underground, using advanced aluminium welding techniques, with vehicle end modules in moulded phenolic resin which has high fire retardency properties.

During 1985 BREL also discussed a number of potential collaboration and joint manufacturing agreements to take the International Coach technology into other markets such as Mexico and China. It is likely that such agreements would bring additional work to Litchurch Lane.

The locomotive works is now (1985) designated as the main bogie manufacturing workshop for BREL, supplying most bogie requirements for rolling stock orders at other works, both for BR and export markets. Considerable investment has brought highly efficient computer controlled equipment into the Works bogie production line.

In addition the Works is responsible for the overhaul of all HST power cars, and for repairs to both Class 45 and Class 20 diesel locomotives and diesel railcar engines, besides remaining available to undertake general engineering work for various customers — not necessarily railway orientated.

Having been established in 1840 the depradations of time and lack of maintenance have taken their toll of the buildings forming the MR complex at Derby. In the station area the housing provided originally by the NMR for its employees in North Street, Midland Street and Railway Terrace began to deteriorate and has only been saved from demolition by the praiseworthy efforts of the Derby Civic Society and the Derbyshire Historic Buildings Trust who took over the restoration of the whole area, with the exception of the Railway Institute, and renovated each dwelling to form very desirable town houses.

With the Midland Hotel which, as previously mentioned, was sold off by British Transport Hotels to the Midland Hotels Ltd, a private company which promptly renovated the interior to something approaching its original style at a cost of some £150,000, the station area was proving to be a conservation area of immense charm.

It is therefore regrettable in the author's view that the British Railways Board found itself unable to carry out a similar exercise on the Derby station buildings which have now largely been demolished to make way for brand new modern station accommodation, thus depriving the conservation area of the most imposing and attractive key feature of the whole ensemble and substituting a building hardly in sympathy with its surroundings, despite the incorporation of large Midland and City of Derby armorial devices in prominent positions on the front of the new main building and retention of the old clock feature, which

has been re-erected on the end wall of the Area Manager's office block at the north end of the station, this work being completed in December 1985.

The first stage of the new station building was due to be completed and opened for use on 6 January 1986, following which most of the remaining part of the old station, comprising the main booking hall, the old 1st class booking hall, ticket and enquiry offices, together with first floor offices, the old Midland Board and shareholders rooms were to be demolished.

It is fortunate that some of the locomotives, rolling stock and other items manufactured at Derby down the years should have been preserved as for example Johnson's 4-2-2 'Spinner' locomotive, No 673 of 1897, and his 4-4-0 Compound locomotive No 1000, albeit as re-built by Deeley in 1914, which now both reside at the National Railway Museum at York along with a finely restored six-wheeled composite of 1884 and other artifacts. At the Midland Railway Centre at Butterley Park in

Below:
The preserved Kirtley 2-4-0 No 158A built at Derby in September 1866 and which is now part of the National Collection, can currently be seen at the Midland Railway Centre, Butterley.
BR Official, Author's Collection

Above:
The original Johnson compound 4-4-0 No 1000, now preserved as rebuilt by Deeley in 1914 and which was built at Derby in 1901 is seen here at Wirksworth. She too is part of the National Collection and can usually be seen on display at the National Railway Museum, York.
BR Official, Author's Collection

Below:
Contrast between old and new at Derby — a modern IC125 set speeds past veteran LMS Class 4F 0-6-0 No 4027 standing on the goods lines just north of Derby Midland station. She too is now part of the National Collection, having been built at Derby in 1924. Photo taken on 27 August 1982. *Ron Jones courtesy* Derby Evening Telegraph

1912 and the historic MR signalbox from Ais Gill, built in the Derby signal works and now restored and re-located in a Derbyshire setting. The Centre also houses LMS and BR rolling stock of all kinds and also locomotives depicting the sequential output of the works at Derby including BR Standard Class 5 4-6-0 No 73129 with Caprotti valve-gear, a Class 11 0-6-0 diesel shunting locomotive and Class 44 1Co-1Co 'Peak' class diesel-electric *Great Gable* dating from 1959. Those in working order operate on the Centre's 3¼-mile line between Hammersmith and Pye Bridge hauling passenger and other trains whilst a major museum is in course of erection for static exhibits.

Almost alone of all important rail centres, Derby remains unaffected to any large extent by the chances and changes of each passing decade, given the inevitable decline in passenger and freight traffic, and remains to this day an important centre uniquely combining both a locomotive works and a carriage & wagon works in association with the Railway Technical Centre in addition to being the headquarters for British Rail Engineering Limited.

Derby has a unique place in railway history which, despite the vast changes in administrations and the tremendous strides in the development of rail transport, deserves to be a secure one, since it has not only proved to be adaptable to the changes required by each successive generation but has, in addition, always been in the van of progress and leading the field in many of the major technological advances achieved during each succeeding decade.

Derbyshire, run by the Midland Railway Trust, many more items of rolling stock are preserved including the Kirtley 2-4-0 No 158A dating back to 1866, a Johnson 'half-cab' 0-6-0T No 1708 of 1880, a further six-wheeler of 1884, the Midland Royal saloon built at Derby in

Appendix: Allocation of Locomotives to Derby at various dates.

Locomotive Allocations

Derby (Midland Railway) December 1880

2-2-2: 1A, 8, 17, 128A, 134A, 135A
2-4-0: 4
2-4-0: 11
2-2-2: 100, 129, 133
2-4-0: 138, 890-899, 1397, 1398, 1478-85
0-6-0: 380, 386, 388, 390-399, 405-9, 411-39,
    1040-1059, 1432-5
0-4-0ST: 1325, 2020
0-6-0ST: 1326 (also shown at Widnes), 1093A
0-6-0T: 1419, 1430, 1431
0-6-0: 257A(?), 381A, 384A
2-4-0: (goods tender), 2017

Derby (Midland Railway) 4 June 1892

2-2-2: 4, 16, 33
2-4-0: 87A, 130-132, 134-136, 138, 139, 890-899
4-4-0: 1566-1571, 1670, 1672
0-6-0: 380, 389-399, 405-439, 484A, 1040-1069,
    1965-1966, 1971-1972
0-6-0T: 1090-1092, 1125-1128, 1973-1982
    (some only)

Derby (Midland Railway) 1 December 1920

2-4-0: 4, 5, 74, 77, 201, 203, 205, 236-9
4-4-0: 328, 488-504
4-2-2: 600, 644
4-4-0: 751, 754, 756, 757, 759-761, 763,
    765-770, 773, 776-779
0-4-4T: 1428, 1429
0-4-0T: 1501, 1512, 1515, 1526, 1527
0-6-0T: 1644-1646, 1795, 1797, 1834, 1839,
    1865
0-6-4T: 2016, 2020
0-6-0: 2401, 2660, 2737-41, 2844/5/7/9/50,
    2852-6/8/9/65/7
0-6-0: 3056/68/88, 3193/6, 3218/9/27/9, 3230,
    3312/15, 95-7/9, 3401/88/89, 3600/3/13,
    3770, 3816-8, 3878-9

Allocated to CME at Derby
0-4-4T: 1210, 1215

Derby (LMS) 5 April 1944

Class 3P 2-6-2T: 111, 174, 193
Class 2P 4-4-0: 378, 406, 407, 418, 513, 516,
    526, 632
Class 3P 4-4-0: 734, 735, 743, 747, 760, 775
Class 4P 4-4-0 Compound: 930, 1000, 1003,
    1033, 1057, 1059, 1060, 1083
Class 1P 0-4-4T: 1240, 1251, 1252, 1337, 1338,
    1368, 1370, 1373, 1404, 1408, 1429
Class 1F 0-6-0T: 1695, 1726, 1754, 1773, 1779,
    1795, 1833, 1847
Class 4P 2-6-4T: 2341, 2509, 2513, 2521, 2523,
    2525, 2527, 2547
Class 5F 2-6-0: 2758, 2774, 2799, 2847
Class 2F 0-6-0: 3045, 3083, 3116, 3123, 3141,
    3175, 3191, 3200, 3264, 3312, 3315, 3353,
    3364, 3368, 3370, 3400, 3440, 3459, 3496,
    3548, 3550, 3584, 3598
Class 3F 0-6-0: 3724, 3735, 3745, 3763, 3776
Class 4F 0-6-0: 4024, 4095, 4136, 4159, 4214,
    4235, 4409, 4419, 4420, 4432, 4475, 4542,
    4565, 4566
Class 5XP 4-6-0 (Jubilee): 5602, 5609, 5636,
    5640, 5649, 5656, 5679, 5696
Class 3F 0-6-0T: 7660
Class 8F 2-8-0: 8008, 8074, 8265
Class 2F 0-6-0: 22849, 22934, 22943, 22958,
    22959, 22982

Derby (BR) 9 September 1950

Class 2P 4-4-0 Compound: 40383, 40404,
    40407, 40411, 40416, 40418, 40426, 40513,
    40632
Class 4P 4-4-0 Compound: 40927, 41000,
    41003, 41023, 41043, 41057, 41059, 41060,
    41084, 41088
Class 2MT 2-6-0: 41247
Class 0F 0-4-0T: 41535

Class 1F 0-6-0T: 41726, 41747, 41754, 41773, 41779, 41795, 41833, 41847, 41889
Class 2P 0-4-4T: 41903
Class 4MT 2-6-4T: 42177, 42340, 42341
Class 5MT 2-6-0: 42847, 42872, 42897
Class 4MT 2-6-0: 43010, 43031, 43049
Class 3F 0-6-0: 43137, 43185, 43191, 43200, 43226, 43259, 43312, 43315, 43318, 43323, 43324, 43361, 43364, 43368, 43402, 43406, 43459, 43469, 43482, 43496, 43510, 43548, 43550, 43572, 43574, 43578, 43584, 43598, 43658, 43735, 43745, 43763, 43776
Class 4F 0-6-0: 43838, 43839, 43840, 43955, 44031, 44142, 44164, 44177, 44402, 44409, 44419, 44420, 44432, 44542, 44565, 44566, 44601, 44602
Class 5MT 4-6-0: 44667, 44776, 44809, 44815, 44818, 44819, 44820, 44847, 44848, 44851, 44917
Class 5XP 4-6-0 ('Jubilee'): 45585, 45602, 45610, 45639, 45656, 45667, 45696
Class 2MT 2-6-0: 46443, 46444, 46454
Class 3F 0-6-0T: 47250, 47417, 47660
Class 8F 2-8-0: 48079, 48121, 48153, 48302, 48390, 48404, 48432, 48640, 48647, 48654, 48677
Class 0F 0-4-0T: 51235
Class 1P 0-4-4T: 58058
Class 2F 0-6-0: 58110, 58125, 58132, 58144, 58148, 58203, 58216, 58246

Derby (BR) 3 October 1964

Class 4 2-6-4T: 42156, 42181, 42225, 42230, 42291, 42610
Class 4F 0-6-0: 44042, 44118, 44214, 44243
Class 5 4-6-0: 44659, 44690, 44804, 44811, 44815, 44830, 44920, 45102
Class 6P/5F 4-6-0 ('Jubilee'): 45667, 45684
Class 0F 0-4-0ST: 47000, 47006
Class 3F 0-6-0T: 47534
Class 8F 2-8-0: 48060, 48064, 48083, 48103, 48124, 48149, 48153, 48170, 48198, 48270, 48284, 48313, 48350, 48359, 48362, 48370, 48510, 48604, 48627, 48635, 48653, 48666, 48704, 48748
Class 4F 0-6-0ST: 68006, 68068
Class 2MT 2-6-0: 78000, 78020, 78021, 78037, 78057, 78064
Type 4 1Co-Co1: D11, D12, D13, D43, D44, D45, D47-56, D58, D59, D78, D80, D82, D83, D85-88, D91, D93, D95-99, D111-125, D127-129, D152, D156, D158, D164
204hp 0-6-0DE: D2377-2383
350hp 0-6-0DE: D3568, D3571, D3587, D3862-3864
Type 2 Bo-Bo: D5188-5190, D5196, D5200, D5205, D5207, D5242, D5246, D5256, D5259, D5265, D5266, D5268, D5280, D5281, D5284-5288, D5290-5297, D7583, D7594
350hp 0-6-0DE: 12033, 12034, 12072

Bibliography

Main sources consulted:

Derby Works and Midland Locomotives by J. B. Radford (Ian Allan Ltd)

A Century of Progress by J. B. Radford (British Railways Board)

Midland Line Memories by J. B. Radford (Midas Books — Baton Press)

A History of the Midland Railway by C. E. Stretton (Methuen, 1901)

Great Northern Lines in Derbyshire (private paper) by G. A. Yeomans

The Derby to Melbourne and Ashby Lines (private paper) by G. A. Yeomans

Midland Railway timetables, leaflets and other documents

LM&SR timetables, leaflets and other documents.

British Railways timetables, leaflets and other documents, and Minutes of the Midland Railway Co; Board of Directors; Way & Works Committee; Locomotive Committee; Carriage & Wagon Committee; Extra Work Books. all held at the Public Record Office, Kew.